The Health of the School Child

Report of the
Chief Medical Officer of the
Department of Education and Science
for the years 1966—1968

LONDON
HER MAJESTY'S STATIONERY OFFICE
1969

SBN 11 270136 1

CONTENTS

CONTENTS

REPORT OF THE CHIEF MEDICAL OFFICER
FOR 1966—1968

To the Secretary of State for Education and Science.
Sir,

INTRODUCTION

This report covers a period of three years instead of the customary two. After the 1964–65 report it was decided to cease publication of a separate report and to use the material in other publications, medical and educational, both to secure wider distribution and earlier publication. When this was announced in 1967, however, there was a widespread appeal especially from educational sources for continuation of the separate report. It is therefore revived, but this report will cover three instead of two years because it was too late to assemble the information for 1966–67 for publication within a reasonable time.

The general findings of the school health service are presented in Chapter I and show that the general standard of health is high. There is, however, good reason to safeguard the nutrition of the boys and girls in those families whose income was estimated in 1967 by the then Ministry of Social Security to be below their assessed requirements. There are no reliable tests of the adequacy of nutrition in marginal cases and preventive action must be based upon accepted standards of minimum requirements and known average food purchases by families of various sizes. Under the auspices of the Committee on Medical Aspects of Food Policy various dietary surveys and other special studies will improve our information in future. Meanwhile, the Department has arranged publicity campaigns to encourage parents who were entitled to free school meals for their children to apply for them.

A substantial minority of the children examined routinely at school entry or selectively later have medical conditions that affect, or might affect, their development and education. These include defects of hearing or vision, physical deformity, asthma, epilepsy, speech and language or emotional and behaviour disorders which may or may not be already known and under medical care. The purpose of the service is not merely to record such defects but to ensure that their impact on the child's education is as innocuous as circumstances allow whether by ensuring treatment or any necessary special educational facility.

Reports in this series have often discussed the merits and demerits of tonsillectomy—the operation most commonly performed on children of school age. Two recent reports mentioned in the first chapter adduce evidence of the real benefit some children receive without as yet defining clearly firm criteria for the selection of those who will benefit. This remains a most vexing problem for general practitioner, paediatrician and otologist alike and one which cannot readily be submitted to ethical clinical trial. The problem of asthma is also briefly discussed and it, too, is currently the subject of investigation because of the increased mortality and hospital admissions during part of the three year period. A numerically, but not proportionately, greater increase occurred at

1

later ages. The situation is improving since precautions over the use of pressure aerosols were suggested by the Committee on Safety of Drugs.

Although the incidence of infestation with head lice has fallen markedly over the years it is still too great and another arthropod household infestation, scabies, has actually increased. These are problems of which the school health service can only see the periphery and their solution depends on other medical and social factors.

The continuing development of child guidance work still falls short of the need and there are wide disparities between areas. Psychiatrists, psychiatric social workers and psychologists are all in short supply, although recruitment has increased steadily. The available psychiatric time has doubled in ten years, but much of the consultants' time is also needed in hospitals. There is similar difficulty in meeting the need for staff in hospital psychiatric units for children and adolescents and in connection with juvenile delinquency. Training posts have been much increased but for the foreseeable future measures which make it possible for the psychiatrist to assist other medical staff in this field will certainly be needed.

The nature and purpose of routine examination of entrants are reviewed in Chapter II. They have changed radically in the past 60 years especially now that all children have easier access to a family doctor under the National Health Service. The function of interpretation of special needs to teaching staff has assumed much greater importance and that of liaison with general practice is simplified where general practitioners play a larger part in this work. Some countries undertake more exhaustive and more frequent examinations but the trend toward a more elastic method of supervision is undoubtedly better in our situation with a different pattern of general practice in support. Some authorities still persist with routine intermediate examinations, a policy which calls for review.

One of the deputy chief nursing officers of the Department of Health and Social Security provides advice to the Department on nursing matters. Miss Lamb has contributed in Chapter III a commentary on school nursing which illustrates the advantages progressively gained from functional unification of health services. At the present time the work of local authority nursing staff is being rapidly regrouped with general medical practices in which nurses are becoming regarded as members of a professional group rather than outside the complement.

Admiral Holgate's review of the dental service in Chapter IV records some improvement in the incidence of dental caries and the progressive increase in the service to children from both the local authority and general dental services. Children in this country undoubtedly have better dental care than at any earlier time, but it is lamentable that they should need so much when the simple procedure of fluoridation of all drinking water could have reduced that need by a half. A quarter of a century after a medical officer of the Department demonstrated the advantages of naturally occurring fluoride in the water and twenty years since the successful demonstration of artificial fluoridation in North America, no more than one child in twenty in this country benefits. By contrast, 75 per cent of New Zealand children now have fluoridated water and already the dental nurse staff requirements have been reduced by one quarter in that country.

2

For many years there has been dispute over the part opticians might play in testing the vision of schoolchildren, and it is satisfactory that in Chapter VI a closer accord can be described. It is less satisfactory that some authorities still do not arrange for testing before the age of 6 or 7 years; three even postpone testing until the age of 8 and some who arrange tests on entry allow far too long intervals before repetition. Co-ordination of this work between education and health authorities and the hospital and specialist services is not yet uniformly satisfactory. The problems of children with both visual and hearing handicaps discussed in Chapter VII are not yet adequately met. Since maternal rubella during early pregnancy may often have been the cause, the current work on rubella vaccines holds out the best hope for the future. Some limited trials of vaccines are in progress.

Medical advances in the last twenty years have prevented most major handicaps from tuberculosis and poliomyelitis in children, but they have also provided means of saving many children with spina bifida who may have major handicaps. Chapter VIII describes the problems emerging for special schools. These may well increase since paediatric surgery is as yet inadequately developed in England and Wales and the provision of more special centres for neonatal surgery is to be expected.

The report for 1935 had a chapter headed 'The Diagnosis of Mental Deficiency'. Chapter IX of this report deals with 'Children who have difficulty in learning'. The difference in approach after an interval of over 30 years reflects the great change which has taken place in the attitude toward children and adults whose mental development is less than average. We now try to keep all who can manage to live with or without support in the community. This chapter emphasises that we are not dealing simply with a single group of abnormalities. Two valuable epidemiological surveys are reviewed and the need for more careful assessment is emphasised.

Health education is a difficult area in which this country lags behind; Chapter X discusses the development in schools and the need for a partnership between the health and educational professions. The Health Education Council was delayed in formation and only established its essential directing staff early in 1969. It should be able to work closely with educational and health staff and, given the necessary funds, put this country into a better position. Effective education on health for young people should not be limited to the problems of drugs, smoking and sex, important as those questions are.

The number of accidents to children in school—estimated in Chapter XI as 3,000 requiring admission to hospital a year—is not large in proportion to the population at risk and the amount of time spent in school.

In recent years it has become plain that although medical diagnosis of disability may be made early in a child's life, the assessment of his physical potential takes longer. Educational assessment often takes longer still and involves teacher, psychologist and school doctor, and frequently one or more medical or surgical specialists, and not least the parents. Much of the early medical assessment of children with severe or moderately severe handicaps is made in hospitals or child welfare clinics and, on the whole, there is satisfactory transmission of information to the school health service. There is need, however, for a closer involvement of the hospital paediatric service in the educational assessment of handicapped children. It would be to the great advantage of

3

handicapped children, to their teachers and their parents (and to the doctors concerned) if the school heatlh service was able to use the type of comprehensive assessment service proposed by a small group chaired by Sir Wilfrid Sheldon whose report was circulated to hospital and health authorities during 1968. Educational assessment requires an educational setting and the presentation of medical factors needs to be made at that point by a doctor with access to both education and health services such as the school medical officer alone has.

If we see in the coming years a functional integration of health services at the local level, this must include greater participation of medical and other professional staff of paediatric departments on the one hand, and groups of general practitioners with their associated nursing colleagues on the other, in the personal preventive services with which school and child health departments have been concerned hitherto. That will be an evolutionary change in which the school or child health service doctor is the essential co-ordinator. There are those who would say that the school health service is approaching its end; they are people without understanding. It is approaching a period of greatly enhanced opportunity closely united with the health provision for children as a whole.

This introduction is a short commentary on the work my colleagues set out in the chapters which follow and I record my thanks to them for the work of the three years it covers. This is the last report in this series which will be edited and partly written by Dr. Peter Henderson who has been Principal Medical Officer (and latterly Senior Principal Medical Officer) in the Department for 18 years. His work is familiar to all who read these reports and to a host of others in this country or abroad concerned in any way with the health of children. In the 62 years since the medical department of the Board of Education was established no one has rendered it greater service.

I am, Sir,
Your obedient servant,
G. E. GODBER

4

CHAPTER I

GENERAL WORK OF THE SCHOOL HEALTH SERVICE

Most school children examined during 1966–1968 were without defects requiring medical treatment or disabilities affecting their education and development. A large minority, however, required the attention of the school health service; in 1967, there were almost half a million with defective vision or squint; over 300,000 with various minor ailments; over 130,000 with orthopaedic defects (mostly minor); and just over 190,000 were verminous (mainly girls with nits in their hair); speech therapy clinics were attended by almost 68,000 and child guidance clinics by over 61,000; over 7,000 were sent for a short period to convalescent homes; over 90,000 were attending special schools or classes, or independent schools taking handicapped children, or having home teaching; and almost 14,000 were waiting admission to special schools; in addition, a large number of children with asthma, epilepsy and physical and other handicaps were in ordinary schools.

School Medical Examinations

In 1967, 1,870,000 children were medically examined at periodic and 1,364,000 at other inspections. The trend—still far too slow—is away from the routine examination of all children in a number of age groups to a more selective system that enables school doctors to spend more time with children (and with their parents and teachers) whose development and education are, or may be, affected by disabilities and handicaps, including those which may arise from divided, broken, or socially deprived homes.

The advantages of a selective system, including the use of screening tests by non-medical staff and questionnaires and letters to parents, were discussed in Chapter III of The Health of the School Child for 1962- 63 so need not be repeated. Most local education authorities continue to arrange for the medical examination of all school entrants and leavers but about half of them have adopted a selective system for children in the intermediate age groups; a few have a selective system for leavers, and one or two are experimenting with one for entrants.

What is essential is that school doctors should review all children after they first start school, taking into account information obtained from parents, teachers, family and hospital doctors, the child health service, and social workers, and paying particular attention to those with medical conditions, or home and social circumstances, that might adversely affect their development and educational progress. Often such an appraisal will not be possible until a child has been at school for several months. Practically all children who are severely, and many who are moderately, handicapped will already be known to the school health service (from reports from the child health service, hospital and family doctors), and will be under its supervision from the day they first start school.

5

There is need for more educational provision for young handicapped children so that they can develop in a stimulating educational environment, where their progress can be assessed by skilled observers—educational, medical and psychological—who, together, can come to an opinion on the most suitable future educational placement of the children.

Medical Record Cards

In November, 1967, a working party of local authority medical officers, doctors from two university departments of social medicine, a paediatrician, and members of the staffs of the Department of Education and Science and the Ministry of Health, with an observer from the Scottish Home and Health Department, was appointed to revise the standard school medical card (Form 10M). The first revision was completed in the autumn of 1968 and the revised form was sent for field trial in a number of areas.

Following a recommendation in the Report[1] on The Handicapped School Leaver, a form of functional assessment for physically handicapped school leavers (Revised Form Y.10) was prepared by a small working party and tried out in a number of areas in 1965–67. It was then amended in the light of the comments received and was ready for general use late in 1968.

Nutrition and School Meals

In 1965, a working party appointed by the Secretary of State for Education and Science reviewed the nutritional standards of the school meal and considered whether the type of school dinner was appropriate in the light of changes in feeding habits since the previous standards were fixed in 1955. It recommended[2] that the total protein content of a school meal should, on average, be 29 grams including, approximately, 18·5 grams animal protein. A school meal should provide a substantial amount of the total daily requirements of protein of children taking school dinners.

From a survey, in June and July, 1966, of 2,683 families with two or more children the then Ministry of Social Security estimated[3] that in Great Britain, in June 1967, there were 487,000 children in families whose resources were below their assessed requirements, and that only 51 per cent of these children over the age of 5 years were receiving free school dinners; 31 per cent paid the normal charges and 18 per cent did not take school meals.

Following the publication of this report, the Department of Education and Science, in November, 1967, issued Circular 12/67 intimating that publicity campaigns were being arranged so that parents who were entitled to free school meals for their children were made aware of their entitlement; and that the arrangements for free school meals would be reviewed to make sure that they did not embarrass children or their parents. A Joint Working Group with local education authorities was set up to consider these matters.

The remission scales for eligibility for free school meals were modified in consequence of the increase in Social Security Benefits from 30th October, 1967, and again in September, 1968. The charge for school meals was increased

---

[1] The Handicapped School Leaver. Brit. Cl. for Rehab. of the Disabled, 1963.
[2] The Nutritional Standard of the School Dinner. Report of Departmental Working Party, 1965. H.M.S.O.
[3] Circumstances of Families. Rpt. of an Enquiry by Min. Soc. Security. 1967. HMSO.

from 1s. to 1s. 6d. in April, 1968, and at the same time children in excess of three in any one family became eligible for free school meals irrespective of their parents' income. (This concession to large families was withdrawn in April, 1969). The arrangements for the remission of school dinner charge were described in Appendix 1 of Circular 11/68 issued on 23rd April, 1968, and amended on 25th September, 1968.

A detailed investigation of the diet, socio-economic circumstances, and clinical condition, including anthropometric measurements, of a sample of children in Kent is being made by Professor Walter Holland, of the Department of Clinical Epidemiology and Social Medicine, St. Thomas' Hospital, in collaboration with the Health and Welfare Department of Kent County Council and the Department of Health and Social Security.

It has to be emphasized, however, that the big majority of school children are well nourished and give no cause for concern.

In the autumn 1968, 5,025,153 children (70·2 per cent of the number present) had school dinners, of whom 840,480 (11·7 per cent of the number present) had them free; 4,181,229 children had school milk. The supply of free milk to pupils at secondary schools and senior pupils in all age schools was discontinued at the end of the summer term, 1968, but continued to be supplied to pupils at primary schools, junior pupils at all age schools and to pupils of all ages at special schools. The percentage of secondary school children taking school milk had decreased steadily in recent years and by the autumn of 1967 only 58 per cent of these children were taking it.

Respiratory and Allergic Disease

Well over 50,000 boys and girls with respiratory disease were under supervision by school doctors. This group of diseases appeared to be more prevalent in some areas than in others. Professor D. D. Reid, in collaboration with a number of principal school medical officers, continued his study of respiratory function and disease in school children in several areas with different degrees of air pollution.

Respiratory disease now accounts for about 8 per cent of the deaths of children, aged 5–14 years, being the fourth most frequent cause of death in this age group (accidents caused rather more than a third of the total deaths, cancer—including leukaemia—20 per cent, and congenital defects about 10 per cent).

The study[4] of 9, 10 and 11 year old children in the Isle of Wight, that was, in part, financed by the Department of Education and Science and the American Association for the Aid of Crippled Children, showed that 2 per cent of them were definitely, and 0·3 per cent probably, asthmatic; more boys than girls were affected; 39·7 per cent of them were in Social Classes I and II compared with 15·7 per cent in the control group; their general intelligence was not significantly different from that of the general population of children; 10·5 per cent of them had 'concomitant psychiatric disorder'.

An earlier survey[5] of children in Birmingham found that 1·83 per cent were asthmatic.

---

[4] Graham, P. J., Rutter, M. L., Yule, W., Pless, I. B. (1967). Brit. J. prev. soc. Med., 21, 78–85.
[5] Smith, J. M. (1961), Brit. med. J., 1, 711.

7

These two surveys suggest that about 150,000 children may have asthma for a longer or shorter period during their school life.

Asthma continued to be the most frequent condition giving rise to admission to the special schools for delicate children. In many it is a serious condition and much more needs to be known about it. Local education authorities provide about 60 clinics for the investigation and treatment of asthmatic school children. A few children are still sent to Switzerland for treatment at a high altitude where they can continue their education.

The number of children dying from asthma increased sharply from 1961 when 30 children in the age group 5–14 years died, reaching 98 in 1967; the number declined to 57 in 1968. There were numerically greater increases at later ages. The causes have not been clearly established but some changes in therapy at that time may have played a part.

Many children have hay fever in the summer months. A survey[6] of 3,958 school children in the Basingstoke area of Hampshire, in 1967, found that 4·1 per cent of them developed hay fever and that half of them had a family history of asthma, eczema and hay fever. Generally the attacks occurred at critical school examination periods and sometimes may have adversely affected the results. There is need for further studies of the educational effects of asthma and hay fever in school children.

Heart Disease

One of the most pleasing features of child health in the past 20–30 years has been the massive reduction in the number of school children with rheumatic heart disease. It is now rare for a child to be admitted to a special school on account of the disease, whereas in 1928 there were over 1,000 boys and girls with rheumatic heart disease in the special schools of London alone. In 1938, 914 children, aged 5–14 years, died from chorea, rheumatic fever and rheumatic heart disease; 11 died in 1966 (6 from rheumatic fever and 5 from chronic rheumatic heart disease).

There are, however, many children surviving with congenital heart defects; over 600 are in the special schools for physically handicapped children.

Otitis Media

In 1908, one in every 60 children examined at school had 'running ears'; among infants the proportion was about one in 30. There was 'evidence of past disease . . . in a considerably larger proportion'.[7] Since then, and particularly in the past 20 years when the school population increased by over 2 million,

---

[6] Roberts, T. E. (1967). The Med. Off. No. 3098, Vol. CXVIII. No. 23. 290–294.
[7] Annual Report for 1908 of C.M.O., Bd. of Education, p. 61. H.M.S.O. 1910.

fewer children were found in school with discharging ears. The figures for 1947–67 are as follows:

TABLE I

Otitis Media

Year	Number of children under or requiring treatment on account of ear discharge	Number of children under observation by school doctors on account of previous ear discharge	Total
1947	17,969	3,923	21,892
1949	19,220	8,312	27,532
1951	15,993	10,610	26,603
1953	16,066	16,362	32,428
1955	12,130	16,011	28,141
1957	10,431	19,243	29,674
1959	11,121	20,817	31,938
1961	9,268	20,068	29,336
1963	9,206	22,385	31,591
1965	9,014	23,707	32,721
1967	8,332	24,035	32,367

The improved general health of children, the reduced prevalence of some infectious diseases, the extensive use of antibiotics, and better facilities for treatment through the National Health Service all contributed to the big reduction in discharging ears among children at school. Since otitis media is a frequent complication of measles it is likely that the number of young children with ear discharge will be reduced still further when the present scheme for vaccination against measles has become fully effective. A reduction in anticipated incidence of measles was already apparent before the end of 1968.

The increasing number of children under 'observation' is an indication of the care being taken by the school health service to prevent impairment of hearing from otitis media, or if it does occur to detect it early.

There are still, unfortunately, some children, particularly those from homes with a poor standard of maternal care, who develop chronic middle ear disease that may lead to impairment of their hearing: it is essential that such children are found early by the school health service and given intensive treatment under the direction of an otologist, to prevent loss, or further loss, of hearing.

Tonsillectomy

Follow-up of school leavers who had tonsillectomy at an earlier age

Mr. T. N. Banham, a consultant ear, nose and throat surgeon, and school doctors employed by the Cornwall Education Authority, surveyed 1,043 school leavers who previously had their tonsils and/or adenoids removed. The majority of the children had the operation at least 5 years before the final school medical examination; the peak age for operation was 7 years; 18 per cent had it after the age of 10 years.

9

The school doctors made a 'careful examination of the upper respiratory tract' and assessed 'the result of the operation in the light of their findings . . . and discussion with the parent . . .'[8] A special record card was designed for the survey on which the parents gave the date of operation, the ear, nose and throat complaints before operation, and their opinion of the result of operation. The hospital case records of 794 of the children were also available.

It was found that 82 per cent were free from symptoms, 14·5 per cent had improved, and 3·5 per cent were unchanged. Only 30 of the 741 children known to have had recurrent tonsillitis before operation continued to have sore throats: the 'vast majority of the parents . . . had no doubt that their children had benefited from operative treatment.'

Mr. Banham thought it improbable that the operation had any influence on frequent colds; he accepted that '. . . symptoms due to adenoids will resolve in time . . .' His conclusion was that 'scientific proof cannot be obtained to give a definite answer to the question: "is the surgical removal of tonsils and adenoids a necessary procedure?" '

Mr. Stuart Mawson and colleagues in the King's College Hospital Group studied[9] a random sample of 404 children in two equal groups. Those in one group had their tonsils and adenoids removed within two weeks of the date the groups were selected whilst operation on those in the other group was deferred for up to two years. The children in both groups were closely followed up when it was found that those in the operated group had an appreciable reduction in the frequency of their attacks of sore throat, tonsillitis, cervical adenitis and colds, and they also gained weight, particularly in the twelve months following operation. There was, however, no significant reduction in the incidence of otitis media, although post-nasal catarrh, snoring and mouth breathing were reduced.

Since about 160,000 children (most of them school children) are operated on annually for removal of tonsils and adenoids further studies are much needed.

Skin conditions, Infestation and Footwear

(a) *Tattooing of Children*

There is some evidence of an apparent increase in the tattooing of children. During a discussion of the subject in the House of Lords[10] on 31st January, 1967, it was mentioned that about 40 per cent of the boys and youths admitted to detention centres and borstals were found to be tattooed.

Dr. A. Lepine, in the first number of the new quarterly bulletin 'Health Trends' published by the Department of Health and Social Security, in 1969, gave the results of an enquiry into the prevalance of tattooing among boys and girls in a sample of approved schools and remand homes. She found that 663 (28 per cent) of the 2,373 boys in 34 approved schools, and 55 (24 per cent) of the 231 girls in 7 approved schools, were tattooed. The big majority of tattoos were self-inflicted; 80 per cent of the girls and 42 per cent of the boys expressed regret at having been tattooed.

---

[8] Banham, T. M. The Journal of Laryngology and Otology. Vol. LXXXII, No. 3. March, 1968. 203–217.
[9] Mawson, S. R., Adlington, P., and Evans, M., J. Laryng., 1968, 82, 963.
[10] Hansard. House of Lords. 1966–67. Vol. 279. 936–950. HMSO.

The practice was briefly referred to by Dr. R. W. Elliott (Principal School Medical Officer, the West Riding of Yorkshire) in the first number of 'Wellbeing' (an excellent, short, quarterly review of health and education written by Dr. Elliott and colleagues in the health and education services of the West Riding), published in March, 1968. Dr. Elliott wrote: 'One West Riding boy had fourteen tattoos on his arms, and another was tattooed from wrist to shoulder. One plastic surgeon reports that he operates on some fifty young people of both sexes each year for the removal of tattoos.'

Self inflicted tattooing (often with needles or pens and marking ink or ink from biro-pens as dyes) is probably as prevalent as that carried out by another person. Despite the obvious health risks of sepsis or infective jaundice from tattooing there is little evidence that these complications often occur. Many of the children, however, when they grow older bitterly regret the disfigurement of tattoos and seek plastic surgery.

(b) *Impetigo, ringworm and scabies*

TABLE II

| | Impetigo | Ringworm | | Scabies |
		Scalp	Body	
1947	64,129	5,454	6,654	38,577
1967	7,972	294	595	11,396

Although many fewer children were treated for these conditions in 1967 than in 1947 the number with ringworm of scalp increased from 137 in 1963 to 294 in 1967, and with scabies from 2,650 in 1957 to 3,499 in 1963 and 11,396 in 1967. These figures are for school children treated through the school health service and not those taken direct by their parents to their general practitioners or through them to hospitals.

The increased prevalence of these two skin diseases shows the need for continued vigilance by the school health service; they must be diagnosed early and treated promptly otherwise they will spread quickly through a class and a school; and often other members of the family are affected.

(c) *Infestation with lice*

It is disappointing that so many children are still found verminous, although the number in 1967 (194,000) was less than a quarter of what is was in 1926 (850,000). The degree of individual infestation is also much less and it is now rare for a school child to be found with body vermin or heavy infestation of head hair. The reduction in infestation has been due to a rising standard of maternal care, improved housing, and persistent, practical health education by school nurses who often visit homes to advise and instruct mothers. There are still many houses without modern facilities and quite a number of inadequate parents; together they largely contribute to the problem of infestation that is, essentially, a family one; the school health service is not alone involved but it must persevere in its efforts jointly with others.

11

(d) *Plantar Warts*

In some areas more children with plantar warts than with any other condition now attend school clinics for treatment. In Southport, 182 boys and girls, out of a school population of about 11,000, were treated for the condition at the local education authority's chiropody clinic in 1967; on average, they each required five treatments.

In York,[11] of 299 children treated at the school clinic by a chiropodist 13 per cent were cured after two, 25 per cent after three, 16 per cent after four, 17 per cent after five, and 14 per cent after six treatments at weekly intervals; 15 per cent took a longer period including two who took 12 weeks to cure.

It is still sometimes asked if barefoot activities during physical education at school are associated with spread of the condition. There is no clear evidence that this is so as a statistical study in the South Essex Division concluded,[12] nor was there a different incidence in boys and girls.

In fact, little, if anything, can usefully be added to the discussion of the subject (so far as it relates to children at school) in Chapter XI, of The Health of the School Child for 1958–59.

Plantar warts are prevalent and troublesome and have a high nuisance value in schools. They present difficult and complex epidemiological and virological problems which merit further enquiry.

(e) *Footwear*

For many years school doctors have reported on the large number of school children, particularly girls, with unsatisfactory footwear, and health education programmes in schools have stressed that the continual wearing of unsatisfactory shoes may cause foot defects, especially in later life.

It is exceedingly difficult to assess the long–term effectiveness of health education, and this is particularly so with health education in school that has to contend with so many adverse influences outside the school. There is some evidence, however, that perhaps rather more children than formerly are wearing shoes of suitable type and size although many still have unsatisfactory footwear.

A survey[13] by a chiropodist of 677 children (357 boys, 320 girls) in three schools in the West Riding of Yorkshire, in 1966, found that 117 (32 per cent) boys, and 94 (29 per cent) girls were wearing casuals, plastic sandals, or pointed shoes or boots; only one child (a boy) wore plimsolls and only two girls wore open heeled shoes; 60 per cent of the boys and 54 per cent of the girls wore shoes of the proper size, of the others 32 per cent of the boys and 39 per cent of the girls had shoes one size too small, and 8 per cent of the boys and 7 per cent of the girls had shoes two sizes or more too small; 18 boys and 16 girls were wearing socks that were too short. The conclusion was: 'On the whole, the type of footwear is more satisfactory than one might have supposed . . . Again, one might have suspected a higher proportion of too short socks . . . it was reasonable to expect a large proportion of shoes regarded as being one size too small. The feet are still growing at a faster rate than the shoes are replaced.'

[11] Shevlin, F. B. The Med. Officer. 7 June, 1968. p. 311.
[12] Leak, W. M. Verrucae Survey in South Essex Division. Annual Report of P.S.M.O. for 1964. pp. 60–69.
[13] Vaines, B. The Chiropodist. Feb. 1967.

This was a useful, though small, survey; too much should not be deduced from it but it points the need for similar surveys elsewhere.

Another indication of the attention now being given to children's feet is that the number of chiropodists employed in the school health service increased from 13 (full-time equivalent about 3) in 1950, to 187 (full-time equivalent about 24) in 234 clinics, in 1967.

Bed Wetters

An increasing number of school doctors are taking particular interest in children at school who continue to wet their beds at night. By January, 1968, local education authorities had provided 162 clinics for the investigation and treatment of bed wetters. Increasingly, also, family doctors refer their school child patients to these clinics. In Cheltenham, for example, most of the boys and girls treated at the local education authority's enuretic clinic were referred to it by family doctors; and one of the consultant surgeons in the town offered to see any child when the school doctor in charge of the clinic thought this necessary.

In Exeter, 6 per cent of the children medically examined when they first started school in 1967 were reported to be bed wetters; in addition, 19 older children with the condition were brought to the school doctors' notice for the first time. Of the 113 children (67 boys, 46 girls), 74 wet the bed every night, 12 on 2–3 nights a week, four once a week and 23 occasionally; 7 children attended the child guidance clinic and one had a urinary tract infection.

Electric alarms continued to be used extensively for children attending enuretic clinics throughout the country. In Exeter, of 26 children who completed using an alarm in 1967, nine continued to have dry beds, seven wet their bed occasionally and 10 showed no improvement six months after returning the alarms to the clinic. Of the 10 who made no progress, two were heavy sleepers; two were emotionally disturbed; one had a congenital defect of the bladder; one was referred to hospital for investigation; two did not use the alarm properly and two failed for no apparent reason.

Enuresis is a troublesome condition. The management of the children is difficult and depends both on the patience and understanding of the parents and on a sympathetic approach by the doctor. There is no single, or certain, method of treatment.

Epileptic Children

About 15,000 boys and girls were under supervision by school doctors on account of epilepsy. Nearly all of them were at ordinary schools; at any one time only about 650 were in the six special schools for epileptic children. Most epileptic children in special schools also have one or more other disabilities, including severe educational retardation, emotional or behaviour disturbance, defective hearing, visual defect, or physical handicap; disturbed adolescents admitted at the age of 13 years or over, whether or not their epilepsy was of late onset, present the schools with their greatest challenge; some require psychiatric treatment in hospital.

Epileptic children may fall behind with their school work and develop psychiatric disorders, particularly of a neurotic and anti-social character more often than non-epileptic children.[14]

Little is known about the special learning difficulties of epileptic children including any which may be due to the effects of anticonvulsant drugs. It has been found[15] that electro-encephalographic manifestations of epilepsy may be associated with interruption of attention of children with classical petit mal, both before and after a fit. Research (financed jointly by the Department of Education and Science and the Gulbenkian Foundation) into various aspects of the learning difficulties of epileptic children is now being undertaken by Dr. C. Ounsted and colleagues in Oxford.

Maladjusted and Psychotic Children and Adolescents

Maladjusted Children

The number of children treated at child guidance clinics almost doubled between 1957 and 1967—from 32,011 in 229 clinics in 1957, to 61,358 in 367 clinics in 1967; psychiatrists employed increased from 195 (whole-time equivalent 66) to 318 (whole-time equivalent 130).

In January, 1968, 4,315 maladjusted children were in special schools, 2,592 in independent schools and 1,695 in special classes in ordinary schools; 1,319 were waiting admission to special schools.

On average, one school child in 124 (1/124 in England, 1/129 in Wales) attended a child guidance clinic in 1967. The ratio ranged from 1/26 in Grimsby to 1/2,108 in Chester and 1/2,953 in Radnorshire (there was a nil return from Solihull). Regionally, it varied from 1/87 in the Southern to 1/238 in the Northern region. Table III gives details.

TABLE III

Number of Pupils, and Ratio of number to total School Population, treated at Child Guidance Clinics in 1967, by Region

Region	Number of Pupils treated at Child Guidance Clinics	Ratio 1:
Northern	2,378	238
Yorkshire (E. and W. Ridings)	5,319	135
North-Western	5,919	185
North Midland	6,511	96
Midland	5,285	159
Eastern	7,664	88
South-Eastern	4,857	102
Southern	6,198	87
South-Western	5,269	98
Greater London	8,363	129
Total England	57,763	124
Wales	3,622	129
Total England and Wales ..	61,385	124

---

[14] Rutter, M. 1967. *Psychiatric aspects of multiple handicap: some epidemiological findings.* Paper read at the Spastics Society Study on Neuro-psychiatry, Alfriston. 1967.
[15] Ounsted, C., Hutt, S. J., and Lee, D. 1963. *Dev. Med. Child Neurol.,* 5, 559.

Within the regions the ratios varied widely in some adjacent or nearby areas: 1/390 in Durham County and 1/1,976 in Northumberland; 1/108 in Newcastle-upon-Tyne and 1/725 in Gateshead; 1/54 in Liverpool and 1/1,078 in Birkenhead; 1/129 in Preston and 1/1,269 in Bolton; 1/142 in St. Helens and 1/1,609 in Wigan; 1/61 in Wolverhampton and 1/804 in Warley; 1/68 in Derbyshire and 1/368 in Leicestershire; 1/50 in Hounslow and 1/510 in Kingston-upon-Thames; in Greater London it ranged from 1/35 in Waltham Forest to 1/510 in Kingston-upon-Thames; in Inner London it was 1/221.

To illustrate these differences in more detail Table IV gives the ratios in the counties and county boroughs of Northumberland and Durham; Yorkshire; Lancashire and Cheshire; Derbyshire, Leicestershire, Northamptonshire and Nottinghamshire; Staffordshire, Warwickshire and Worcestershire. (It also gives the ratios of children treated by speech therapists.)

TABLE IV

Ratio of Pupils treated at Child Guidance Clinics and by Speech Therapists in a number of areas, 1967

Areas	Treated at C.G.Cs. Ratio 1:	Treated by Speech Therapists Ratio 1:	Areas	Treated at C.G.Cs. Ratio 1:	Treated by Speech Therapists Ratio 1:
North Eastern			*Lancashire and*		
Northumberland	1,976	106	*Cheshire*		
Durham	390	184	Lancashire	559	151
Newcastle-upon-Tyne	108	135	Cheshire	343	139
Darlington	59	347	Liverpool	54	402
Gateshead	725	194	Manchester	115	75
Hartlepool	606	82	Barrow	577	189
Middlesbrough	133	97	Birkenhead	1,078	165
South Shields	139	211	Blackburn	205	69
Sunderland	104	119	Blackpool	146	157
Tynemouth	544	74	Bolton	1,269	133
			Bootle	390	640
			Burnley	318	86
Yorkshire			Bury	151	60
East Riding	669	132	Chester	2,108	1,505
North Riding	266	165	Oldham	121	110
West Riding	174	247	Preston	129	884
Leeds	132	246	Rochdale	225	126
Sheffield	67	220	St. Helens	142	258
Bradford	222	372	Salford	193	73
Kingston-upon-Hull	295	252	Southport	133	243
Barnsley	175	49	Stockport	84	182
Dewsbury	27	25	Wallasey	110	66
Doncaster	107	67	Warrington	327	87
Halifax	63	88	Wigan	1,609	348
Huddersfield	121	63			
Rotherham	128	85	*Midland*		
Wakefield	138	115	Staffordshire	331	99
York	62	132	Warwickshire	106	85
			Worcestershire	147	205
			Birmingham	285	379
North Midland			Coventry	127	194
Derbyshire	68	271	Stoke	114	88
Leicestershire	368	282	Burton	1,470	48
Northamptonshire	132	34	Dudley	287	104
Nottinghamshire	124	109	Solihull	—	80
Derby	77	144	Walsall	371	110
Leicester	88	114	Warley	804	120
Northampton	262	209	West Bromwich	74	228
Nottingham	91	128	Wolverhampton	61	169
			Worcester	156	—

Frequently stated reasons for paucity of child guidance clinic facilities are shortage of psychiatrists and geographical and environmental areas unattractive to professional staffs. Neither of these reasons can adequately explain the disparity in the number of children treated at child guidance clinics in some of the geographically adjacent areas listed in Table IV.

There is, undoubtedly, a shortage of psychiatrists, psychologists and social workers. In 1968, the Summerfield Committee[16] reported on psychologists in the education service and the Seebohm Committee[17] on the personal social service. A leading article in the British Medical Journal,[18] when discussing mental health services for children, suggested that 'Paediatricians and school medical officers are also more likely to see disturbed children than the specialised psychiatric services, but are often reluctant to attempt to deal with these problems because of their uncertainty about their own capacity to offer effective treatment and because of lack of available psychiatric consultation . . . it would seem that child psychiatrists have an enormous responsibility for education and consultation. Perhaps they should sacrifice some of the pressures and satisfactions of individual therapy and spend more time giving training, consultation, and support to colleagues, both medical and non-medical, who are providing individual and family care in the community.'

In fact this proposed procedure had already been adopted by one or two local authorities. In some areas where it had been found impossible to obtain the services of a sufficient number of psychiatrists, senior and experienced school doctors, after attending various courses on the emotional and behaviour difficulties of children and having assisted a psychiatrist for a period in a child guidance clinic, became responsible for the medical work in some child guidance clinics, consultant psychiatric advice being available for specially difficult cases. In the West Riding of Yorkshire, in 1968, two senior medical officers, who had received in-service training, were responsible for the psychiatric work in two child guidance clinics; two medical officers were having in-service training with a view to their promotion to senior clinical medical officer for work in the child guidance service. A course for medical officers on handicapped children, including maladjusted children, one day a week for an academic year, was also started. In the West Riding, as in a number of other areas, doctors with the Diploma in Psychological Medicine, but not having a hospital appointment as a consultant psychiatrist, were employed in the local education authority's child guidance service. A married woman doctor who had ten years' experience as a psychiatric registrar was also employed for eight sessions a week. Similar arrangements could well be made in other areas.

Psychotic Children

It was estimated[19] from a survey of children, aged 8–10 years, that there might be about 3,000 autistic children of school age in England and Wales.

Psychotic children, including those described as autistic, are difficult to place in school both on account of their behaviour and their special learning

---

[16] Psychologists in Education Services. The Summerfield Report. H.M.S.O. 1968.
[17] The Seebohm Report on the Local Authority and Allied Personal Social Service. H.M.S.O. 1968.
[18] Mental Health Services for Children. British Medical Journal (1967) No. 5552. Pp. 585–586.
[19] Letter, V. 1964. Early Childhood Autism. Ed. Wing. J. K. The Commonwealth and Internat. Library: Robt. Maxwell.

difficulties. By April, 1968, there was a small amount of special provision for them in 17 hospital schools, in 3 day units in hospitals, in 17 day units not attached to hospitals, in two special schools for psychotic/austitic children, and in three independent schools. Some psychotic children were in special schools for educationally subnormal or maladjusted children; an unknown number were in local health authority training centres and in hospitals for the severely subnormal.

There is need for more facilities for autistic children and for study of the effect of different forms of medical and educational treatment on their behaviour and on their social and educational development. Several new units are being prepared, and others planned, by hospital and local education authorities either individually or jointly. Dr. M. Rutter, of the Institute of Psychiatry at the Maudsley Hospital, with financial support from the Department of Education and Science, is investigating the progress of autistic children in three different educational environments.

Seriously Disturbed Adolescents

There is widespread shortage of medical and educational provision for severely disturbed adolescent boys and girls. Under the London Boroughs Association an interested group established themselves as a working party in December, 1965, under the chairmanship of Dr. F. R. Dennison, Medical Officer of Health and Principal School Medical Officer, Newham, to consider the needs of seriously disturbed children and adolescents in the Greater London area. An interim report[20] was prepared for and adopted by the Association in October, 1967. One of the main recommendations of the report was that the Department of Education and Science, the Home Office, the Ministry of Health, the Consultative Committee of the four Regional Hospital Boards serving Greater London, the Inner London Education Authority and an appropriate London borough, should be consulted with a view to a pilot survey being made to assess the needs of disturbed adolescents in Greater London and to provide co-ordinated services for them in a suitable area within Greater London. The Boroughs of Newham and Tower Hamlets were finally selected for the pilot study.

Children with Speech Disorders

The number of school children treated for defective speech increased from 49,187 in 1957, to 67,894 in 1,420 clinics, in 1967. This increase was not due to more children having defective speech but to more treatment facilities for them: 652 (whole-time equivalent 434) speech therapists worked in the school health service in 1967 compared with 379 (whole-time equivalent 355) in 1957. On 31st December, 1967, there were still about 200 vacancies for speech therapists in the school health service.

A training school for speech therapists was opened by the Leeds Education Authority in 1966 and by the Birmingham Education Authority in 1967. In addition to these two new training schools there are four in London and one each in Leicester, Manchester and Newcastle-upon-Tyne (the only one in a university); there are also two in Scotland.

---

[20] Interim Report of the London Borough Association Working Party on the Provision for Seriously Disturbed Adolescents. 1967.

On average, one school child in 112 (112 in England, 105 in Wales) was treated by speech therapists in 1967; the ratio ranged from 1/84 in the Southern Region to 1/166 in the East and West Ridings of Yorkshire.

There were wide differences in the ratios not only between but also within regions. In English counties the ratio ranged from 1/34 in Northamptonshire to 1/602 in Westmorland; and in English county boroughs from 1/25 in Dewsbury to 1/1,505 in Chester. In Wales, the range was from 1/44 in Cardiganshire to 1/886 in Carmarthenshire, and from 1/57 in Merthyr Tydfil to 1/621 in Newport (Mon.).

There were surprising differences in the ratios in some comparable and adjacent areas—1/34 in Northamptonshire and 1/282 in Leicestershire; 1/85 in Warwickshire and 1/205 in Worcestershire; 1/56 in Surrey and 1/127 in Kent; 1/82 in Buckinghamshire and 1/164 in Berkshire; 1/133 in Bolton and 1/884 in Preston. Table IV shows the differing ratios within a number of regions. Some northern areas had as much as or more provision than some southern ones—for example, the ratio in Lancashire (1/151) was practically the same as in West Sussex (1/152) and higher than in Worcestershire (1/205); in Cumberland (1/62) it was twice as great as in Kent (1/127) or Inner London (1/124).

Some therapists give more time to children with severe disorders of speech and less to those with simple defects of articulation and, in consequence, treat fewer children. Increasingly, too, the language disorders of children are becoming the concern of therapists who are thus brought straight into the field of work of teachers. Indeed, it is often difficult to distinguish between 'therapy' and 'teaching'. Partly on account of this the Secretary of State for Education and Science, the Secretary of State for Health and Social Security, and the Secretary of State for Scotland had under consideration the appointment of a committee 'To consider the need for and the role of speech therapy in the fields of education and of medicine, and the assessment and treatment of those suffering from speech and language disorders and the training appropriate for those specially concerned in this work and to make recommendations.'

Follow-up Study of School Entrants who had Defective Speech
Chapter V of The Health of the School Child for 1964–65 gave the results of a survey, by Dr. Esther Simpson, one of the Department's senior medical officers, of the speech of five year old children at school in Leicester in 1965; 54 boys and girls (2·7 per cent of entrants) were found with a significant speech defect. On re-examining 42 of the 54 children in the summer term of 1968, Dr. Simpson found that 19 (11 boys, 8 girls) had achieved normal speech, of whom six had a reading age two years or more below their chronological age; nine (4 boys, 5 girls) still had a slight speech defect, of whom four were two or more years retarded in reading; 14 (10 boys, 4 girls) continued to have a significant defect of speech, eight being two or more years retarded in reading.

Follow-up Study of Children discharged from a Special School for Children with Speech Disorders
A study[21] of 49 boys and girls discharged to ordinary schools from the John Horniman School for children with speech disorders, brought to light some

---

[21] Griffiths, C. P. S. John Horniman School. Rpt. on Follow-up of Children who left the school between July, 1958, and June, 1965. Invalid Child. Aid Assoc. 1968.

18

unsatisfactory circumstances. Although full reports on each child had been sent by the John Horniman School to the local education authorities concerned the teachers of some of the children had not been told that they had been to a special school on account of defective speech and language. Some children who had been recommended for continuing speech therapy had not received it. The speech therapist from the John Horniman School who made the study considered that some of the children were under strain and were not making the educational progress expected when they left the special school; she thought that this might have been due to a child's language development being less advanced than it appeared to be at the time of discharge from the special school.

This study brought out clearly the need for adequate information being given to teachers in ordinary schools about children in their classes who had been at special schools and who were in continuing need of observation or treatment. It is the responsibility of the school health service, as well as of the local education department, to ensure transmission of relevant information between special and ordinary schools.

The study also showed that boarding schools themselves have a responsibility for preparing the children they intend to discharge to ordinary schools for life in these schools—a way of school life that is often more strenuous than that in a residential one.

Immigrant Children

Some local education authorities require the medical examination of immigrant children before their admission to school in order to ensure that any needed treatment is given. This can generally be arranged, including X-ray examination of lungs, within a week.

Medical examination before going to school is generally accepted and usually welcomed by the parents of immigrant children. In Bradford, for example, there were only three objections to this procedure out of some 4,000 children examined.

On account of the high rate of respiratory tuberculosis that had been found in adult male immigrants, children before starting school usually had a Heaf skin test and, if necessary, an X-ray examination of their lungs; up to 50 per cent of them were tuberculin negative and were offered B.C.G. vaccination.

Parasitic infection of school entrants varied with their country of origin; about 18 per cent had hookworm, whipworm, round worm or tapeworm. In Bradford, with the consent of the general practitioners concerned, children with parasites were treated at the school clinics. Their standard of cleanliness was usually good.

Many of the children were smaller than those born in this country but few showed signs of serious malnutrition; about 3 per cent were severely anaemic; only an occasional one had rickets.

Some required education in special schools for the physically handicapped on account of paralysis from poliomyelitis contracted before coming to this country.

Immigrant children need to feel at ease and secure in school and this depends largely on the attitudes of the teachers, school health service and other staff,

19

and on a good relationship between them and the parents. The crucial importance of confidence and understanding between the parents and doctors, nurses,
teachers and others cannot be over-emphasized. It is essential that the latter
know something of the social and religious customs of the children, particularly
girls, since many of them come from countries where the emancipation of
women is still at an early stage. Different attitudes towards clothing, changing
for physical education, diet and other personal problems should be recognised,
and sufficient time should always be allowed for children to adjust to the often
very different social circumstances and customs of their new environment.

There are also the problems of communication. Many immigrant children
have little or no knowledge of the English language when they arrive in this
country; if they continue to talk to each other in their own tongue they will be
slower in learning to speak English. A child from a home where English is not
normally spoken starts with a language handicap that impedes his adjustment
into British school life. As with all children, native or immigrant, behaviour
problems may follow if difficulty with language is not promptly recognised and
dealt with. When an immigrant child is suspected to be educationally or severely
subnormal it is essential that time should be allowed for adjustment to the new
environment before any definite assessment is attempted, and when this is
done it may be necessary to enlist the help of an interpreter.

Special Educational Provision for Handicapped Children

Examining handicapped children and those suspected of being handicapped,
recommending (in collaboration with educational colleagues and after consideration of reports from hospitals, general practitioners and social workers) the most
suitable educational provision for them, keeping them under supervision whilst
at ordinary or special schools, and advising their parents, now absorb much of
school doctors' time. On 1st January, 1968, over 90,000 boys and girls were
receiving special education and over 10,000 were waiting admission to special
schools.

Table V gives the number, and number per 10,000 school population, of
handicapped children who were receiving special education, or were waiting
admission to special schools (excluding children in hospital schools) in England
and Wales, and also by region, on 1st January, 1968. Table VI gives the number
of special classes in ordinary schools and the number of children attending
them.

TABLE V

(i) Number of handicapped children receiving education in special schools, independent schools, special classes and units; boarded in homes; receiving education in hospitals and at home in accordance with Section 56 of the Education Act 1944; and awaiting admission to special schools in January 1968. (Children receiving education in hospital special schools are not included).*

(ii) Incidence of above per 10,000 school population.

Region	School Population	Blind (i)	Blind (ii)	P.S. (i)	P.S. (ii)	Deaf (i)	Deaf (ii)	Pt. Hg. (i)	Pt. Hg. (ii)	P.H. (i)	P.H. (ii)	Del. (i)	Del. (ii)	Mal (i)	Mal (ii)	E.S.N. (i)	E.S.N. (ii)	Epil. (i)	Epil. (ii)	Sp. Def. (i)	Sp. Def. (ii)	All Handicaps (i)	All Handicaps (ii)
Northern	567,678	115	2·30	148	2·96	277	5·54	206	4·12	988	19·76	548	10·96	324	6·48	4,741	94·82	75	1·50	14	0·28	7,436	148·73
Yorks E. & W.R.	719,959	143	2·00	237	3·32	393	5·50	320	4·48	1,183	16·56	909	12·73	618	8·65	4,962	69·47	89	1·25	23	0·32	8,877	124·28
North Western	1,095,291	209	1·88	308	2·77	477	4·29	554	4·99	1,797	16·17	2,030	18·27	1,041	9·37	10,468	94·21	188	1·69	30	0·27	17,102	153·91
North Midland	631,158	100	1·60	153	2·45	325	5·20	211	3·38	753	12·05	412	6·59	593	9·49	4,584	73·33	45	0·72	18	0·29	7,194	115·10
Midland	844,034	135	1·62	371	4·45	374	4·49	403	4·84	1,544	18·53	1,450	17·40	739	8·87	7,307	87·68	89	1·07	14	0·17	12,426	149·12
Eastern	673,375	87	1·30	136	2·04	224	3·36	346	5·19	730	10·95	505	7·58	1,140	17·10	4,424	66·36	74	1·11	19	0·29	7,685	115·28
South Eastern	498,795	93	1·86	109	2·18	207	4·14	297	5·94	591	11·86	546	10·92	1,171	23·42	3,671	73·42	42	0·84	24	0·48	6,751	135·06
Southern	540,006	82	1·64	96	1·92	129	2·58	314	6·28	681	13·62	391	7·82	975	19·50	4,018	80·36	59	1·18	30	0·60	6,775	135·50
South Western	516,689	75	1·43	103	1·96	202	3·84	279	5·30	699	13·28	413	7·85	667	12·67	4,225	80·27	43	0·82	17	0·32	6,723	127·74
Greater London	1,083,833	187	1·68	477	4·29	620	5·58	681	6·13	2,266	20·39	2,501	22·51	3,796	34·16	9,495	85·46	115	1·04	21	0·19	20,159	181·43
Total: England	7,170,818	1,226	1·72	2,138	2·99	3,228	4·52	3,611	5·06	11,232	15·72	9,705	13·59	11,064	15·49	57,895	81·05	819	1·15	210	0·29	101,128	141·58
Wales	468,435	70	1·47	109	2·29	108	2·27	314	6·59	515	10·82	264	5·54	349	7·33	2,347	49·29	23	0·48	5	0·10	4,104	86·18
Total: England & Wales	7,639,253	1,296	1·68	2,247	2·92	3,336	4·34	3,925	5·10	11,747	15·28	9,969	12·96	11,413	14·84	60,242	78·31	842	1·09	215	0·28	105,232	136·80

*In addition, 3,873 children were being taught in hospital schools.

TABLE VI

Special Classes and Units in Ordinary Schools, January, 1968

Category	Number of Classes	Number of Pupils		
		Full-time	Part-time	Total
Delicate	12	141	—	141
Maladjusted	159	620	1,075	1,695
Partially-Hearing	215	1,498	221	1,719
Partially-Sighted	15	105	2	107
Physically Handicapped	35	220	89	309
Total	436	2,584	1,387	3,971

There were considerable variations in some of the percentages of children receiving special education in the different regions, and, indeed, within a region; circumstances accounting for these variations included: shortage of specialist staff, insufficient provision of special schools and classes, and different ascertainment rates that, at least to some extent, reflected different views on what constituted a handicap or disability necessitating the children being taught in a special school or class.

In addition to the children included in Table V, 3,873 others were being taught in 91 hospital schools. Among the children included in Table V were those in 192 other hospitals who either formed too small a number, or were not in hospital long enough, to justify the provision of a special school, but for whom local education authorities provided teachers; in 135 of these 192 hospitals the number of children taught ranged from 1–9; in 41 from 10–19; in 14 from 20–29; and two had over 30.

In the past 20 years approximately 2,500–3,000 children were reported annually, under Section 57(4) of the Education Act, 1944, to the local health authorities as unsuitable for education at school, 2,624 were reported in 1967. During this period there was increasing pressure for the transfer of responsibility for the education and training of severely subnormal children from the health to the education services. On 26th November, 1968, the Prime Minister announced in the House of Commons that the Government had decided, after considering the views of the local authority, professional and other organisations it had consulted, ' . . . to accept in principle that responsibility for the education of mentally handicapped children should be transferred from the Health to the Education Service.'

Child Care Staff in Special Schools
On 1st January, 1968, there were 2,687 child care staff in boarding special schools; 277 of the 321 men and 1,783 of the 2,366 women had no professional training of any kind. Among those with professional training were 194 nurses of whom 127 were State Registered, 57 were State Enrolled and 10 were Registered Sick Children's Nurses.

Medical Staffing of the School Health Service
On 31st December, 1967, 2,914 doctors (full-time equivalent 930), excluding consultants, were employed in the school health service; only 153 were engaged

as full-time school doctors; 1,813 were in full-time local authority service, giving part of their time to the school health service (in total, this amounted to the equivalent of 624 full-time doctors); and 948 were general medical practitioners or married women doctors working part-time as school doctors (equivalent full-time 152). There were vacancies for the full-time equivalent of 150 doctors; local education authorities also had increasing difficulty in finding suitably experienced doctors for posts in the senior medical officer grade.

General practitioners and married women doctors have been employed in the school health service almost since it first started but it is only in the past few years that substantial numbers have been engaged in it—618 in 1964 and 948 in 1967. The work of general practitioners in the school health service was discussed in Chapter XIV of The Health of the School Child for 1964 and 1965. Since then the trend towards greater use of their services has continued and now about one school doctor in three is also a family, or a married woman, doctor.

There is also need for a much closer working relationship between the school health and hospital paediatric services, especially in the medical care of handicapped children.

The work of school nurses is considered in Chapter III and of school dentists in Chapter IV.

CHAPTER II

THE MEDICAL EXAMINATION OF
SCHOOL ENTRANTS

During 1969 a number of local authorities will be using on a trial basis a revised draft of the school medical record Form 10M that was prepared by a Working Party set up for the purpose. One of the features of the new draft is that, on the page recording the findings at the examination, the items against which entry is required reflect principally the nature and extent of the examination of a school entrant. Over the years when periodic medical examinations have been changing in character and frequency and children in junior and secondary schools have been selectively invited to attend for medical re-examination, there has been universal agreement on the need for routine examination of all children on entry to school. In fact, there is wide acceptance of the need for entrant examinations to be particularly searching and comprehensive when re-inspection of all children at certain ages is no longer the rule.

When the school health service was inaguarted a circular[1] was issued to local/education authorities giving general guidance on the aims of the service. The purpose of school medical inspections was defined then as 'the medical examination and supervision not only of children known, or suspected, to be weakly or ailing, but of all children in the elementary schools, with a view to adapting and modifying the system of education to the needs and capacities of the child, securing the early detection of unsuspected defects, checking incipient maladies at their onset, and furnishing the facts which will guide Education Authorities in relation to physical and mental development during school life'. For the first twenty years or so, checking 'incipient maladies' was a major task of the service, but by 1931 it had begun to take on the preventive role that its designers had always foreseen as being necessary and appropriate. That year, three reports drew attention to the physical health of children in the years immediately preceding entry to school and to the appreciably higher prevalance of disease and physical defects among school entrants than older children. At the same time the Chief Medical Officer to the Board of Education noted[2] that 'the whole trend of modern medicine (was) the early detection of the beginning of disease and the fortifying of the normal person.'

Although the prevalence of incipient maladies, disease and disorders is with few exceptions still highest among school entrants the general level of physical health in school children of all ages has improved so much during the last 35 years that the question may well be asked: how far are school medical examinations today performing the other functions mapped out in 1907—functions the continuing need for which still remains the justification for the service?

---

[1] Circular 576, Board of Education, 1907, H.M.S.O.
[2] Report of Chief Medical Officer, Board of Education, 1931, H.M.S.O.

The 'examination and supervision of children known, or suspected to be, weakly or ailing'—in modern parlance, the identification, assessment and continuing care of handicapped pupils—has progressed until it is now a major function of the school health service rather than routine medical inspection. Most children handicapped by severe mental, physical or sensory disorders are brought to the notice of the school doctor before they enter school. But these children constitute a minority of the handicapped pupils who are already receiving special education in special schools. The majority is made up of children with similar, though usually rather less severe disabilities (particularly among educationally subnormal and maladjusted pupils) for whom special education is provided at a relatively late stage in their primary school years. Furthermore, for every child in a special school there are approximately another ten in ordinary schools with moderate difficulty in learning or problems in social and emotional adjustment. These are all children who now require from the school health service 'the early detection of unsuspected defects' and for whom the education system needs 'adapting and modifying' and the education authorities (and it might be added today—parents) need furnishing with '. . . the fact which will guide (them) in relation to physical and mental development during school life'.

There is great need to help these children before their difficulties lead to frustration and educational failure. This means they need to be identified if possible when they first come to school, and their teachers and parents advised from that time. In effect, this calls for no more than a logical extension of the work of the school health service into the very field of primary prevention for which it was conceived, albeit in relation primarily to mental development. Such an advance is likely to reap a rich reward for individual children and the community alike, and at present no better instrument exists for achieving this than the school entry medical examination, suitably modified for the purpose.

The Medical Examination

The main objective of the school doctor at the entrant medical examination is the recognition of conditions which may interfere with a child's normal development and learning in school.

According to their mode of action such conditions may be rated as direct or indirect. Direct factors may interrupt the basic sequence of learning and behaviour by disturbing either sensory function, the processes within the brain or motor responses. Indirect factors may interrupt the opportunities to learn by causing absence from school (as from illness), or by causing disturbance in a child's motivation to learn (such as social and emotional maladjustment, general mental or physical malaise, or lack of parental interest in education).

The entrant medical examination has traditionally centred on a search for physical factors directly affecting vision, hearing, and the quality of movement (and posture), and on indirect physical factors of both a general and more specific kind (e.g. general physical condition and defects of the heart or lungs). Too little attention has been paid to primary mental or neurological factors affecting the learning processes and to secondary factors of a non-physical kind that disturb motivation. It is a matter for regret that the study of these factors has been relatively neglected at a time when developmental assessment has

25

been accepted as an integral part of the doctor's examination of the infant and toddler. There is no logical reason why this should cease to apply when a five-year old child is examined on entry to school.

An important—though by no means the only—reason for this is the tendency for the behaviour and problems of children to be thought of as mainly physical or mainly mental, with the corollary that the principal role of the school doctor is to take care of the physical aspects (especially if he is not trained in child psychiatry). An arbitrary differentiation such as this may be reasonable when growth and development are being described or discussed, but if carried too far in medical and educational practice it is all too easy to lose sight of the fact that the seat of mental processes in the physical structure of the brain which must be intact not only for normal thought to take place, but for it to be seen to have occurred. This is true for behaviour, too. We readily equate intellect with 'grey matter'. The brain is also the substrate of personality, a point obscured by contemporary writers.

The difficulty arises here that the physical integrity of those parts of the brain and central nervous system concerned with learning cannot be checked, clinically, without recourse to mental tests and for school doctors to apply such tests as a routine might be regarded by some as trespassing in the province of the psychologist. There is a good deal of overlap, however, between the disciplines of neurology and psychology, especially in five-year old children whose intellectual development is passing, at varying rates, from the sensory-motor phase to that of intuitive thought and higher cognitive skills. Unless this is realised and accepted there is a danger that the overlap may become a gap and certain areas of behaviour crucial to learning in school may be omitted from the study of young school children, particularly since they do not receive routine psychological examination. One of the responsibilities of school doctors is to watch over the assessment needs of the child as a whole.

The doctor's examination and assessment of a child on entry to school must start with a physical examination geared to detect abnormalities in physical structure of importance to learning. In doing this it is only reasonable to take the opportunity to look also for significant medical conditions (e.g. undescended testes, hernia, etc.) which may have no bearing on a child's education in school. But the examination should be related to function, and 'function' should include mental function.

For this reason developmental and neurological tests should be included in the entrant medical examination as an additional screening technique. They do not need to be applied to children with clearly recognisable signs of neurological disorder (such as cerebral palsy, spina bifida) since these children automatically require comprehensive examination and assessment. Nor are they likely to reveal unequivocal evidence of serious neurological disorders previously unsuspected. Their purpose is to give a broad assessment of certain aspects of cerebral function crucial to a child's learning and behaviour.

The complexity of human behaviour is such that is is exceedingly difficult to test separate components of cerebral function in isolation. Many of the tests available test more than one function (e.g. tests of dexterity concurrently test visuo-motor co-ordination). For the purpose of screening neurological function in a young child—i.e. establishing whether behaviour and learning have reached a level of proficiency consistent with the developmental norm

26

appropriate for the child of a given age—this relative non-specificity is no serious draw back. By selecting certain tests it is possible to screen some of the most important components of neurological function.

At present, no short battery of screening tests exists that has been standardised and validated for English five-year old children and that can be applied within an acceptable length of time for the examination of a school entrant. But school doctors could apply selected tests from among those already available and themselves study the subject further. The response of the child to these tests will need to be interpreted against a background knowledge of what may be accepted as normal for a five-year old child. The presence of more than one equivocal sign, especially if these are accompanied by a suspicious peri-natal or medical history or by concern on the part of the teacher, would then be a signal for less hurried and more comprehensive medical and psychological examination in the school doctor's clinic. The interpretation of neurological signs then confirmed may call for referral to a consultant neurologist.

If the examination to the school entrant is to include such screening, time must be allowed for this in scheduling the medical examination. In practice, it has been found that an average of 15 minutes per child is sufficient to obtain a medical and developmental history and to carry out a physical examination and neurological and developmental tests of sensory-motor function. It is not possible for a doctor to carry out more than a cursory physical examination if he is scheduled to examine eighteen to twenty infant school children in a session of $2\frac{1}{2}$ hours. A higher priority should be given to arrangements which ensure that every child receives a careful and comprehensive screening examination on entry to school than to those that attempt to arrange for each child to receive three medical inspections of the traditional kind during his school years. Such entrant examinations then provide a sound basis from which a school health service may confidently proceed to rely upon selective medical examinations for the subsequent identification of children needing medical supervision.

The Parental Questionnaire

A parental questionnaire is an essential pre-requisite to the doctor's examination. The examination itself may well reveal signs that lead to a decision to re-examine the child in six to twelve months' time, not only or necessarily because of uncertainty about the signs, but because of a known association between such signs and later learning difficulties. The peri-natal and past medical histories may add significance to the signs or they may themselves contain factors known to predispose the child to behaviour and learning problems later. Experience has shown that 'at risk' registers cannot (and it was never anticipated that they could) be relied upon to lead to the discovery by the age of five of all children with minimal or moderate disabilities affecting development and learning; a screening-type examination is essential. Nevertheless, the concept of some children being at risk in their development is valuable in alerting doctors to children who may need to have a special watch kept on their development for one reason or another. Enquiry of parents regarding certain medical events since birth supplement 'at risk' registers.

Time is precious in an entrant school medical inspection. A parental questionnaire is no more than a highly effective time-saving device when the parent and child are with the school doctor; it can very quickly indicate to the doctor areas of special interest that must be pursued personally with the parent. It cannot replace all the questions that the doctor needs to put to the parent about the health of the child.

Two features of the peri-natal history are particularly important; birth-weight and length of gestation, that give information about prematurity and immaturity at birth. A history of cerebral injury or infection is clearly important, as is also the occurrence of fits or fainting that may be epileptic in origin. A history of middle-ear infection should be sought, and the parents asked if they have ever thought the child might have had any difficulty in seeing or hearing. It is useful to know whether the parents consider their child is clumsy in loco-motion or manipulation, or presents any problem in management at home. Appropriate questions should be included about a delay in the child's use of speech, or delayed speech or difficulty in learning to read on the part of any relative on either side of the family. A family history of epilepsy or asthma may also be relevant.

Communication with Teachers and Parents

It is common practice for the school doctor to discuss with the head teacher or class teacher his findings at the entrant examination. The completion of a form summarising his findings for the teachers is no substitute for a discussion. It is often claimed that there is no time for discussion, either because the doctors have a very tight schedule or because the teachers cannot leave their children unattended, and many head teachers of infant schools have their own class. The doctor's schedule can be adjusted if some priority is given to the examina-tion of school entrants. Teachers usually welcome a doctor in the classroom when such a visit allows them to express their concern or satisfaction with certain children, or to demonstrate a child's difficulties in a group learning situation. A child who had been shy in the strange setting of a medical inspection may be more relaxed when with his friends in the classroom and the doctor may be able then to make a better assessment of his speech. To see the group together busy or otherwise in their classroom, whilst the teacher talk about each one examined (or to be examined) is an advantageous situation in which to obtain the teacher's assessment of adjustment and response to education. The sharing of observations about children in this way may be as valuable as the exchange of information. A school doctor cannot afford to dispense with the observations of, or discussions with, teachers about children who for one reason or another do not conform to rule.

Three comments may be made about the information that school doctors can give to teachers. The first concerns the explanation of medical terms and conditions. Nowadays, many people not trained in medicine (and especially teachers of primary school children) have a modicum of knowledge of medical matters. This is usually superficial and whilst it is sufficient to sharpen their interest when a child in their class has a particular condition it is usually neces-sary for the doctor to correct misconceptions and to explain what the condition really means and how it affects the child.

Epilepsy affords a good example of such a condition. Most teachers are vaguely aware that epilepsy has something to do with convulsions. It is rare to find one who is familiar with the other multifarious manifestations, and it is not at all uncommon to find that although they have been told by a parent or

28

doctor that a child has epilepsy they have not been told what happens to that particular child when he does have a seizure. It still happens that teachers are not informed that a particular child is subject to epilepsy. Since teachers have responsibility for pupils whilst they are in school it is manifestly not fair either to them or to the child that this information is withheld and they are not advised how to deal with the child in the event of a seizure.

The second point about communication with teachers concerns the effect a condition may have on a child's behaviour and learning and the kind of information they need to help them teach that child. For instance, it is important enough to tell a teacher that a child is subject to momentary episodes of loss of attention associated with petit mal, but if she is told that the child's inattention may extend for short periods associated with abnormal electrical impulses before and after an obvious 'absence' she will be more understanding of the child's disadvantage and better informed to adjust her teaching to compensate him.

The school doctor can be of great help initially to teachers of children with minimal cerebral dysfunction. Teachers are frequently the first to appreciate that there is something about many of these children that 'doesn't make sense'. Without knowing exactly why, they are yet aware of certain inconsistencies in either behaviour or performance not entirely explained even by a measure of intellectual retardation when this is present. From the extended developmental and neurological screening the doctor may not be able to give the teacher a detailed report, but he will have been able to form a shrewd idea of the general nature of the child's difficulties. The teacher will find it reassuring that her 'hunch' about the child was correct. The understanding that follows from this glimpse of the etiology leads to a more rational approach to management even if specific advice about teaching methods has to wait upon the results of a more comprehensive examination.

The third point about communication with teachers concerns the expectations they have of their pupils. Dealing as they so often do with many children within a narrow age band in large classes, it is understandable that there should be a general tendency on their part to expect all school entrants to behave like an average five year old, particularly when the child appears physically normal and not so mentally retarded that this is obvious at the outset. But the rate of growth varies very considerably among children of a given chronological age and even in the same child progress in development is seldom steady and equal in all fields. Many prematurely born children by the age of five have not fully made up in stature for their short gestation, and neurological maturation may be equally delayed for their age though not necessarily for their total life span. A sound opinion derived from developmental and neurological screening that a child is less mature in growth and development than average for his age will be readily heeded by a teacher. The greater understanding the teacher gains about the child results in a lowering of the pressure on the child to conform to the average in performance, and in the adoption of expectations of the child that are more consistent with his individual characteristics and circumstances.

This kind of outcome is just as much to be sought for the child at home as in school and may be achieved by giving the parents greater insight into their child's capabilities and personality. An interpretation of what a defect means to the child when in school may reassure the parents about the school's management and teaching of the child. Children who are just below the average in their performance often need protecting from the ambitions their parents have for them,

c   29

especially when their problems are related to specific learning difficulties rather than a more general intellectual retardation. The association between learning difficulties, particularly with reading, and problems in behaviour is well known; timely advice to parents as well as to teachers on the management of such children may forestall later disturbance in emotional development.

The value of the school entrant examination is enhanced for all children if the school doctor discusses with the parents the intellectual and emotional development of their child. However, in doing so, the doctor should not overlook the value to the parent of an independent opinion that their child is physically normal and healthy. The school medical examination is also a rare opportunity for health education, which is likely to be the more effective if the parent has a special concern for the physical health and care of her child and about which she seeks advice.

CHAPTER III

THE SCHOOL NURSING SERVICE

During the years under review there have been advances in the organisation of the school nursing service similar to those made in the community nursing services. Much thought has been given to the adoption of modern methods of organisation in order to provide a better service for both the child and the school and to use available manpower in the most efficient manner. The school nurse and doctor have been partners since the start of the service in 1907, and during these sixty years there have been many developments in the school health service which have affected the work of the school nurse.

The concept of the school nurse/health visitor was strengthened by regulations made under the Education Act of 1944 and by the National Health Service Act of 1946. Regulation 54 of the Handicapped Pupils and School Health Service Regulations, 1945, required (subject to saving clauses for existing staff and for nurses employed solely in school clinics, in boarding special schools, or on specialist duties) that all school nurses should, in future, be qualified health visitors. This was designed to facilitate the co-ordination of school and maternity and child welfare nursing services, and to secure continuity in the nursing supervision of pre-school and school children, in areas where there were separate school and maternity and child welfare services. Increasingly, the school nurse has become the friend and adviser of the child, teacher, and parents, thus strengthening the links between home and school.

The function of the school nursing service is still to provide services for both the child and the school, and to maintain a health link between the school and the home. In carrying out her functions the health visitor/school nurse maintains continuity of supervision by making regular and frequent visits to the school, and in consultation with the teacher she is able to identify children in need of medical examination, and to give particular attention to the detection of certain defects, especially early defects of vision and hearing and abnormalities of behaviour. The link between the school and the home is maintained by the health visitor/school nurse carrying back and relating to the home the findings in school, and by her seeking to remedy any adverse factors which may be contributing to deviations from health. Since the family doctor must be concerned also, the development of attachments to practices has added completeness to the liaison and improved the effectiveness of work.

In the report of the Central Advisory Council for Education (England) published in 1967 mention was made that the improvement in the health of young children during the last thirty five years had been tremendous. Reference was also made to the appointments of health visitor/school nurses and that this combination of functions helped them to fulfil their function so that their sphere of work was broadly based and able to extend to the whole family.

In practice it has been found that the contribution of the health visitor/ school nurse is particularly useful in nursery, primary, and junior schools, but that difficulties sometimes arise in secondary schools where children come from a wide catchment area and from homes which are not known to the health visitor/school nurse of that particular school.

The following table shows the total nursing staff employed in the school health service between the years 1951 and 1967, the increased number employed with the health visitors certificate and the increase in the number of nursing assistants.

TABLE I

Year	Total Number of Pupils on Registers of Maintained and Assisted Primary and Secondary Schools (including Nursery and Special Schools)	Total School Nurses	Whole Time Equivalent of school Nurse	Number with H.V. Certificate	Number of Nursing Assistants
1951	5,799,619	5,411	2,517	3,624	318
1958	6,914,291	6,721	2,599	4,992	409
1962	7,044,977	7,449	2,667	5,749	507
1965	7,181,416	8,129	2,835	6,121	627
1967	7,428,593	8,823	2,889	6,215	569

It is important to ensure that proper use is made of the experience and skill of the health visitor/school nurse and that consideration is given to the use of ancillary staff in the school nursing service. In 1965, the Minister of Health recommended to local health authorities the report of a sub-committee of the Standing Nursing Advisory Committee on the extent to which the local authority nursing team could be developed and its effectiveness increased by the use of ancillary help.

Although this report and Circular 12/65 under which it was issued related to the community nursing services, some consideration was also given to the use of ancillary nursing staff in the schools. This is particularly important as there is an overall shortage of health visitors for work in the schools and for general duties with the local health authority. The report described the nature of duties that were undertaken in the school nursing service and also considered how these duties could be delegated without affecting the quality of the service to the child.

The report stated that 'the health visitor should lead the nursing team in the School Health Service as in the Local Health Authority Service and should similarly be supported by state registered nurses and lay assistants. She should work closely with parents, class teachers as well as head teachers, other officers of the education authority and with school doctors and general practitioners. Much of the home visiting in connection with school children will need to be done by her. We think she should be present at the medical examination of children on first entry to school but it will be more economical of her time to consult with the school doctor and school teacher before or after other routine medical examinations. We do not think that she need normally attend any of the clinics provided under the School Health Service. She should play an active part in health education, particularly of the young'. A number of Principal School Medical Officers have discussed this subject in their annual reports.

In one London Borough (Newham) where there was difficulty in recruiting health visitors it was decided to delegate as much work as possible in schools to state registered nurses, with the health visitors maintaining overall responsibility for the work. The state registered nurses were allocated a number of schools and worked in close co-operation with the health visitor responsible. The health visitor carried out the functions described in Circular 12/65 and the state registered nurse attended at periodical medical inspections, undertook health surveys which included hygiene inspections and routine vision testing.

In the county of Surrey state registered and enrolled nurses are employed on a part-time basis to relieve health visitors of routine medical inspection duties in secondary schools and at school clinics operated independently of infant welfare centres. This enables the health visitors to devote more time to health education in schools and to make better contacts with head teachers to discuss health problems, while following up in the home of children found to have defects at medical and hygiene inspections still remains an important part of their duty. The sessions worked by part-time nurses and the fixed appointments of the health visitors are illustrated in the following tables.

TABLE II

A. Part-time School Nurses Sessions Worked in 1967

	Preparation for Medical Inspection	Medical Inspection	General Medical Clinics	Immunisa- tion	Other	Total
Total	103	1,158	1,327	1,010	473	4,071

B. Health Visitors' Fixed Appointments in 1967

	Prepara- tion for Medical Inspection	Medical Inspection	General Medical Clinics	Hygiene	Teaching Sessions	Others	Total
Total	759·5	1,432	445·5	294	394·5	618	3,943

Commonwealth Immigrants

The arrival of immigrant families into this country has increased the work load in some areas of the school nursing service. The most difficult problem is one of communication, particularly with the Indian and Pakistani women whose knowledge of English is extremely poor. In one county borough twenty health visitor/school nurses volunteered to learn Urdu, and in one London borough a school nurse was appointed who was able to speak Hindu and Urdu. This nurse was able to give great assistance to teachers, medical officers, and the families concerned. She was able to help the parents understand facts relating to personal hygiene, immunisations and many other matters.

Local authorities with a high immigrant population try to provide an increased number of health visitor/school nurses and supportive staff. In one such authority the teachers have spoken of the invaluable help that they have

33

received from health visitor/school nurses who have knowledge of the homes of these families.

Health visitors and school nurses are also used in obtaining information on the number of immigrants and children of school age who are resident in the area of the local authority.

Health Education

Health visitors receive increasing requests for help in health education in schools. Such help can either be provided by the health visitor actively participating in the school health education programme or by her assisting in the preparation of a syllabus. Health education in schools provides learning experiences for influencing attitudes, knowledge, and conduct relating to personal and community health.

In one county where health visitors have participated in health education programmes within the schools syllabus since 1959, the role of the health visitor is described as that of a skilful group leader. She tries to lead and inspire the thoughts and conversation of the young people, thus helping them to form and think out right decisions on the basis of thought for others.

In another local authority area health visitors take full advantage of opportunities to meet boys and girls in talks and discussions on health topics; during 1967 they gave talks in every secondary school on the hazards of smoking cigarettes.

School health education is becoming an integral part of education for living as a whole, and the health visitor/school nurse has an important role in it.

In-Service Education

In order to provide a better service for children and to use professional staff in the most efficient manner, it is necessary for local authorities to arrange in-service education and training for them. Such training is required for nurses who join the school nursing service and have not trained as health visitors, and on going in-service education is required for all employed in the school nursing service. This ensures that all are kept aware of the needs of school children and the developments and advances within the school health service. In-service education has the advantage of being flexible and capable of adaptation according to local needs.

In Berkshire a course of training is organised for school nurses who do not have the health visitors certificate. The course is organised on a day release system and lasts for fifteen weeks. During this time visits of observation are arranged and lectures given on the following subjects:—

1. *Social Services*

   Emphasis is given to the development and legislation of education and school health services.

2. *Study of children*

   Physical, emotional and intellectual developments
   The normal child
   The child at risk
   The child requiring special education.

34

3. *Responsibilities of the School Nurse*
   Screening tests
   Routine observation tests
   Practical techniques
   Liaison with health visitors and other agencies
   Organisation of work
   Methods of prophylaxis
   Infection in schools
   Follow up of defects found in children
   Verminous children, general survey and legislation
   The child in the nursery
   Relationship with auxiliary workers.

4. *Health Education*
   Use of displays in school premises
   Individual health education
   Informal talks to classes of young children
   Planning a syllabus
   Series of formal talks to classes of young children
   Use of visual aids.

5. *Changing Needs of the School Child*
   Current medical problems concerning the child
   Current social problems and their implications for the school child.

The London Boroughs Training Committee also arrange an introductory course for school nurses at regular intervals. This course is specially designed for clinic nurses who are going to undertake school nursing duties. The London Boroughs Training Committee arrange the lecture days and the practical work is arranged by the individual boroughs concerned. The course is of two weeks duration, four days of which are spent at lectures and the remainder gaining practical experience.

The programme for 1968 included the following:

LECTURES: The education system of England and Wales
The health of the school child
Personal hygiene and the conduct of general surveys
Control of communicable diseases in schools
Assessment of need for special education
The school nurses work in special schools
The relationship between the school health and other health and welfare services.

35

FILMS: 'I want to go to school'
              'The happy adventure'
              'Growth and development of children'

DISCUSSIONS: Organisation of a practical problem at the school medical
              examination
              Demonstrations of some practical procedures in school nursing
              work
              Practical problems arising in 'follow up' and treatment
              Final discussion at the conclusion of the course.

SYMPOSIUM: Health Education in different types of schools.

Future Developments

In the report on the Health of the School Child for 1964 and 1965 it was stressed that the future of the school health service lies in a closer working partnership with the consultant paediatric and general practitioner services, with the teacher and parents, and in the assessment of how children function in school rather than the routine examination of all children in an age group—other than school entrants—irrespective of their needs.

The future of the school nursing service also lies in a closer working partnership with the family doctor services thus helping towards a closer working partnership with the Hospital based services. Health visitors have traditionally brought to the school health service a knowledge and understanding of children's early health and development and of their family backgrounds. As the health visitor may be in touch with the child from birth, in nursery care and later at school she is able to participate in the on-going assessment of children and particularly with the handicapped child.

There has been a steady development of attaching health visitors and nurses to doctor's group practices thus fusing these services to meet modern needs. Such attachments ensure that doctors, health visitors and nurses are able to work as true partners within the groups so providing a community health team. This concept is helping to bring the school nursing service closer to the general practitioner service.

In Cumberland where all the domiciliary nursing staff are attached to doctors group practices a fresh approach has been tried where general practitioners and attached staff have been introduced into the school health service. It is probably too early to assess accurately how this is working out in practice, but it is interesting to note some of the comments that have been made. The headmaster of a junior school has found that co-operation and ease of contact has improved, leading to a friendly, easy approach between school, parents and all medical, dental, welfare and nursing staff. It has been found that parents feel more at ease with one of the group of doctors, whom they know already and that a relaxed parent communicates this feeling to her child. The close contact between the health visitor, general practitioner and school is useful and the accessibility of the health visitor has often solved problems. Her knowledge of local conditions has helped the school, the children's officer and school welfare officers.

A nursing officer in the same county was concerned that the attachment of health visitors and nurses to general practitioners complicated the work of the health visitor in the school health service. It is inevitable that several health visitors cover the catchment area of even the smallest schools. Where however the general practitioner is also involved in the school health service the continuity of care and supervision is maintained.

The aim of modernisation is to provide a better service for children and schools and to ensure that maximum use is made of available staff. The concept of the community health team working within the school health service requires further experiment; it would appear to lead to a more integrated and better personal service.

CHAPTER IV

THE SCHOOL DENTAL SERVICE

The Staffing Situation

At the end of 1967 there were 1,821 dental officers employed in whole or part time duty within the local authority dental service and this represented a whole time equivalent of 1,364 dental officers of whom 1,272 were working within the school dental service. These numbers show a marginal increase in staff but the actual improvement in the staffing ratio in terms of dental officers to children is offset by the increase in the school population. There has however been a welcome increase in the number of dental auxiliaries within the service. The number of general dental practitioners in contract with executive councils increased by 45 in 1967, and as this was the first significant increase since 1962 it can be said that the increase in the number of local authority dental officers bears a favourable comparison. There has been an increase of 25 per cent in the number (full time equivalent) of school dental officers since 1959 as against an increase of 7 per cent in the number of dentists on the Register of the General Dental Council. The increases in numbers on this Register follow the recent enlargement of dental schools. The number of dental auxiliaries within the local authority service had increased to 162 by December, 1967, and preliminary returns in December, 1968, showed that 87 authorities were employing almost 200 dental auxiliaries. In future the auxiliary will play an important role in the dental service of any local authority which conscientiously seeks to carry out its commitments. There is an insufficient number of dentists and better use of ancillary staff provides the best prospects for controlling dental disease in the children treated by the school dental service. These girls are proving a useful addition to the service and they have been readily accepted by both staff and the children they treat; in many areas where there is an insufficient number of dental officers the additional assistance has been invaluable.

In March, 1968, the Ancillary Dental Workers Regulations were laid before Parliament and these become law on the 1st September, 1969. The dental officer directing the dental auxiliary must now prescribe in writing the specific treatment to be provided for the patient and this represents a major change in the regulations. In a statement to the House of Commons the Minister of Health made the distinction between direction and personal supervision when he said: ' "Direction" enables a dental officer to assess, in the light of personal knowledge of the auxiliaries in his team, the degree of supervision each one needs, varying from the very close supervision that a recently qualified and inexperienced auxiliary clearly must have to the minimum essential direction required by a skilled and experienced auxiliary. It would be wasteful and uneconomic to apply the same rigid standards to all regardless of individual skills and reliability.' The Minister's guidance should assist the directing officer and prevent the wastage of valuable clinical time within the service.

The distribution of dentists throughout England and Wales is uneven and the inability of an authority to maintain an adequate complement of dental officers influences the pattern of treatment which it is possible to provide. Dentists are motivated by a variety of reasons in seeking employment in a particular local authority. Even the dental surgeon who is aware of the importance of children's dentistry and imbued with the desire to treat children may well shrink from undertaking services in the unsatisfactory drab environment tolerated by some authorities in previous decades. Attractive well equipped premises enhance the reputation of the service and parents, children and dental staff derive mutual benefit. It is pleasing to record that a great number of well equipped modern clinics exists within the service. A graded staffing structure will attract staff who intend to make their career within the local authority service and many authorities have created higher posts in order to give experienced dental officers greater responsibility and this has resulted in a corresponding improvement in their staffing situation.

Over the past ten years the pattern of treatment has markedly improved. Conservation is now readily accepted by the great majority of parents and their children. In any area dental treatment for children can be provided by the local authority or the general dental service. The number of children which the general dental practitioners are willing to treat can materially affect the demands on the school service. If the demands on the school service are too great a poor pattern of treatment will result but if it can be modified by the general dental service contribution the dental officer will have the opportunity of providing more sophisticated treatment. The general dental service is treating an increasing number of children and the improvement is reflected in the national statistics. Whilst only 7 per cent of all courses were provided for children in 1949–50 this figure had risen to 29 per cent of full courses in 1967.

The value of commencing regular dental inspections at an early age is now generally recognised. The importance of examining new entrants to a school can scarcely be overstressed, for it may be their first contact with the dentist and the advice given to parents at this stage may well lead to dental care being accepted throughout life.

Quinquennial Survey of the Incidence of Dental Caries

In 1968 a dental survey of 5-year-old and 12-year-old children was undertaken by school dental officers. This was the fifth survey in a similar series; previous ones were carried out in 1948, 1953, 1958 and 1963 in the same areas in Manchester, Middlesex, Northumberland, Nottinghamshire, Somerset, West Riding of Yorkshire and East Sussex.

The London Boroughs of Barnet, Brent, Ealing, Hillingdon, Hounslow and Richmond-on-Thames co-operated in the study preserving the continuity in that all these authorities were previously within the boundary of the former local authority of Middlesex. The number of children examined was substantially the same as those examined in the previous studies and similar clinical and sampling procedures as before were adopted.

Average figures for d.e.f. (i.e. decayed, extracted and filled deciduous teeth) and D.M.F. (i.e. decayed, missing and filled permanent teeth) were obtained for both 5 and 12 year old groups. In addition the number of 5-year-old and 12-year-old children with no d.e.f. or D.M.F. teeth was expressed as a percentage

39

of the sample. Prior to 1968, only the returns from Northumberland County Council have expressed the number of decayed, missing and filled teeth separately and the more detailed statistics consequent on this practice are shown as a graph in figures 4 and 5.

This year separate returns for decayed, missing and filled teeth have been obtained for all areas and for the first time the pattern of treatment in the various authorities can be demonstrated. (Table II).

The results show that there has been a general improvement in the dental health of the schoolchildren in the regions in which the survey took place and this general trend could not have been anticipated with certainty in 1963, although improvement in the dental state of five year olds had already begun to show. The percentage improvement in the number of children with no d.e.f. teeth was 4·2, bringing the total to 21·6 per cent which approaches the 1948 figures when the effect of sugar rationing was thought to be a factor worthy of consideration in the figures for that year. The average number of decayed, extracted and filled teeth decreased by 0·6 which is the same decrease as was recorded for the five year period ending in 1963.

There was an increase of 1·3 per cent in the number of 12 year old children who had no D.M.F. teeth and the average number of D.M.F. teeth had decreased by 0·1 per child. It is particularly satisfying to note these improvements because the dental state of the 12 year old deteriorated rapidly between 1948 and 1952. The number of D.M.F. teeth did not increase in the five years from 1958 to 1963 at the same rate as it had in previous quinquennials and in the years 1963–1968 a small reduction had been demonstrated. From figures 1–4 it appears that 1958 represented a turning point in the dental state of schoolchildren and these statistics are supported by those provided by Northumberland County Council. The sugar consumption in 1958 was 121·9 lbs per head of population which still is our highest level.

The consumption of sugar in 1967 which has been provisionally estimated at 115·7 lbs per head per annum is still high and may be related to a high prevalence of caries. The improvements recorded may be due to health education carried out by the staff of local authorities and others which may be eliminating the more harmful dietary habits and fostering the sound maxims which assist the child to achieve dental health.

TABLE I

(a) 5 Year olds

Area	Number of children examined	Number of children showing no d.e.f. teeth	Percentage of children showing no d.e.f. teeth
Manchester ..	838	168	20·0
Middlesex	1,607	500	31·1
Northumberland ..	4,599	784	17·0
Nottinghamshire ..	649	186	27·1
Somerset	2,500	531	21·2
West Riding ..	4,569	967	21·2
East Sussex ..	1,019	283	27·8
Total	15,781	3,419	21·6

(b)   12 Year olds

Area	Number of children examined	Number of children showing no D.M.F. teeth	Percentage of children showing no D.M.F. teeth
Manchester ..	795	55	7·0
Middlesex ..	1,579	79	5·0
Northumberland ..	4,162	196	4·7
Nottinghamshire ..	632	34	5·3
Somerset	2,500	125	5·0
West Riding ..	4,304	206	4·8
East Sussex ..	918	59	6·4
Total	14,890	754	5·1

TABLE II

(a) 5 Year olds

Area	Total number of d.e.f. teeth	Total of d teeth	Total of e teeth	Total of f teeth	Average number of d teeth per child	Average number of e teeth per child	Average number of f teeth per child	Total of d.e.f. teeth
Manchester ..	3,654	2,291	972	391	2·7	1·2	0·5	4·4
Middlesex ..	5,938	3,371	713	1,854	2·1	0·4	1·2	3·7
Northumberland	23,464	14,387	6,395	2,682	3·1	1·4	0·6	5·1
Nottinghamshire	2,079	1,331	324	424	2·0	0·5	0·7	3·2
Somerset ..	11,465	7,249	1,948	2,268	2·9	0·8	0·9	4·6
West Riding ..	20,319	14,533	4,253	1,533	3·2	0·9	0·3	4·4
East Sussex ..	3,851	2,554	369	928	2·5	0·4	0·9	4·8
Total	70,770	45,716	14,974	10,080	2·9	1·0	0·6	4·5

(b)   12 Year olds

Area	Total number of D.M.F. teeth	Total of D teeth	Total of M teeth	Total of F teeth	Average number of D teeth per child	Average number of M teeth per child	Average number of F teeth per child	Total of D.M.F. teeth
Manchester ..	3,568	1,079	676	1,813	1·4	0·8	2·3	4·5
Middlesex ..	8,557	2,290	559	5,708	1·5	0·3	3·6	5·4
Northumberland	22,376	7,012	3,160	12,204	1·6	0·8	2·9	5·3
Nottinghamshire	3,097	1,350	535	1,212	2·2	0·8	1·9	4·9
Somerset ..	12,522	3,639	1,116	7,767	1·5	0·4	3·1	5·0
West Riding ..	27,035	10,867	2,791	13,377	2·5	0·7	3·1	6·3
East Sussex ..	4,669	1,144	276	3,249	1·2	0·3	3·6	5·1
Total	81,824	27,381	9,113	45,330	1·8	0·6	3·1	5·5

TABLE III

Sugar consumption per head in the United Kingdom
Total (sugar content) gross, including Honey and Glucose

	lbs		lbs		lbs
Pre-war	106·4	1949	97·5	1959	117·5
1940	80·3	1950	89·7	1960	118·5
1941	72·3	1951	99·1	1961	120·3
1942	72·3	1952	94·4	1962	117·9
1943	71·9	1953	104·5	1963	118·8
1944	76·9	1954	111·7	1964	115·0
1945	73·8	1955	114·5	1965	116·2
1946	82·4	1956	115·9	1966	117·4
1947	87·2	1957	118·2	1967	115·7
1948	88·3	1958	121·9		

Fluoridation of Public Water Supplies

Whilst the Department of Education and Science is not concerned with the measures taken to fluoridate water supplies, the effect of fluoridation will be much to the advantage of the school dental service. Schoolchildren in Birmingham, Newcastle and Gateshead, along with those in parts of Warwickshire, Worcestershire, Durham, Northumberland and Yorkshire are now drinking water which has been fluoridated and the preliminary surveys on Birmingham 3 year old children demonstrate a significant improvement in the state of their dental health. A measure which reduces the need to fill millions of teeth annually deserves maximum support from all dental officers who are in a strong position to advise their authorities of the great benefits which will accrue from it. Dental officers who have examined children in fluoridation areas will have noted the strikingly good appearance of the teeth.

The report on fluoridation studies in the United Kingdom and the results achieved after 11 years was in draft form in December, 1968; it confirmed the findings of the 1962 report in the study areas. There is a substantial reduction in the amount of decay in temporary teeth and fluoridation has a similar benefit on permanent teeth. The complete safety of fluoridation has been confirmed and its adoption by local authorities is strongly to be encouraged.

Dental Health Education

Dental health education was being carried out as effectively as present knowledge permits in many areas and it would be invidious to single out one particular authority. The methods and techniques employed ranged from the modest efforts of some to the large campaigns of others. Staffing and other facilities influenced the action taken in this field.

The campaigns which were commenced by four local authorities in 1962 were completed in 1966 and the results seemed less impressive than was anticipated despite the great effort by the staff. The general impression was that the campaign did have some effects but these were transitory and that it was easier to reinforce an existing trend than to break new ground. Children were readier to clean their teeth immediately after meals rather than clean them more often. The improvement in d.e.f. and D.M.F. teeth as measured by the examining dental officers was not significant. The results show that a sensitive method of evaluation is difficult to devise. The dedicated field worker expects no quick return from his efforts and the improved national picture as seen in the quinquennial survey may be attributed to an improvement in standards due to dental health education. Dental health education will form an integral part of the work of the new Council for Health Education which took over the responsibilities of the former Central Council for Health Education and some of the activities of the Ministry of Health in 1968. The central responsibility for health education now lies with the new Council and dental officers requiring advice about carrying out local health education programmes should contact that body.

Recent Departmental Action

This chapter does not list all the agreements reached in the last three years or describe in detail even the more recent circulars pertaining to the service, but a brief mention of some may be helpful. Circulars 23/66 of the Department of Education and Science and 22/66 of the Ministry of Health issued in December, 1966 described the steps taken by the Secretary of State for Education and Science and the Minister of Health to meet the criticisms made of the local authority dental service in the First Report of the Estimates Committee, 1962–63. The circulars intimated the appointment of joint dental staff and the action taken by them. The joint dental staff have now visited all local authorities in England and Wales, the great majority of them more than once. The visiting officer reports on the proper development of the service and the pattern of treatment being carried out by the authority's dental staff, the condition of premises, plans for their improvement or reconstruction and the dental provision in future building. Equipment is assessed as to its suitability; the orthodontic service and the development of programmes on dental health education are also reviewed by the visiting officer. An official letter (or letters) on behalf of the two Secretaries of State is sent to the authority after such a visit and this letter may recommend specific actions which may be taken to improve the authority's dental service .

In August, 1967, the Minister of Labour advised his colleagues at the Department of Education and Science and the Ministry of Health that he intended to regard the Factories Act 1961 as applicable to dental laboratories. This action was taken in the light of the result of the appeal to the House of Lords in the case of Haygarth v. Stone, 1965; in view of this local authorities were advised to contact H.M. Factory Inspectorate to request that dental laboratories be visited and that they be advised on the measures to be taken which would bring them into line with the Act.

Circulars 7/67 and 39/68 of the Ministry of Health dealt with health centres. The number of centres is increasing and they provide accommodation for the medical and allied professions. Many of the new centres include dental accommodation for local authority staff and so facilitate greater integration and co-operation between local authority dentists and their colleagues in the general dental service, all of them serving in a team for the benefit of the community.

Handicapped Children

The dental care of mentally and physically handicapped children has been receiving increased attention within the local authority service during the past few years. These two groups present the service with a problem disproportionate to their numbers, particularly in areas where it has proved difficult to give adequate dental care to the normal child population. The treatment of most handicapped children requires a great deal more time and trouble than that of normal children; they obtain less than the usual amount of treatment from the general dental service for a variety of reasons and because of this some local authorities have developed a treatment service for them.

In the past the treatment of handicapped children by local authority dental officers was, through force of circumstances, too often restricted to extractions only, mostly under general anaesthesia for the relief of pain and the elimination of sepsis. Local authority dentists are concentrating increasingly on conservative dental treatment for these children. In some areas routine visits are now being made to every training centre or arrangements are made on behalf of these children with a regional hospital board. Many mentally handicapped children are at present in junior training centres or in hospitals for the severely subnormal. When the junior training centres become the responsibility of the local education authorities the whole range of the authorities' school health including the school dental services will be available to the children attending them everywhere; but this arrangement is already in force in a number of areas.

General Anaesthesia

In 1967, a report on General Anaesthesia in Dentistry by the Joint Sub-committee set up by the Standing Medical and Dental Advisory Committee of the Ministry of Health was published by H.M.S.O. It gives valuable advice on the selection of patients for general anaesthesia and the precautions which should be taken for their safety. In view of the increasing number of immigrant children who are seeking treatment from the local authority dental service the possibility of sickle call anaemia or other blood abnormalities in patients of African descent should be borne in mind. In such children it would seem wiser to replace general by local anaesthesia, unless this possibility has been excluded.

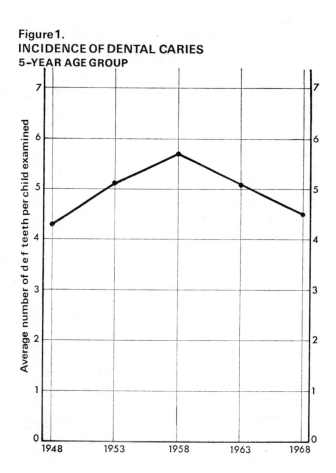

Figure 1.
INCIDENCE OF DENTAL CARIES
5–YEAR AGE GROUP

Figure 2.
5-YEAR AGE GROUP

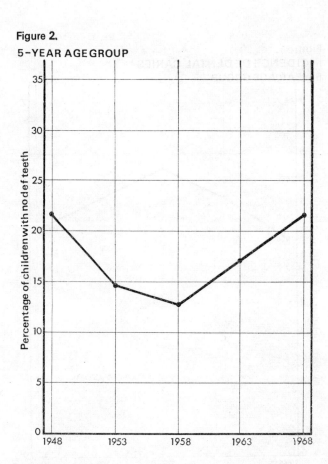

Figure 3.
INCIDENCE OF DENTAL CARIES
12 -YEAR AGE GROUP

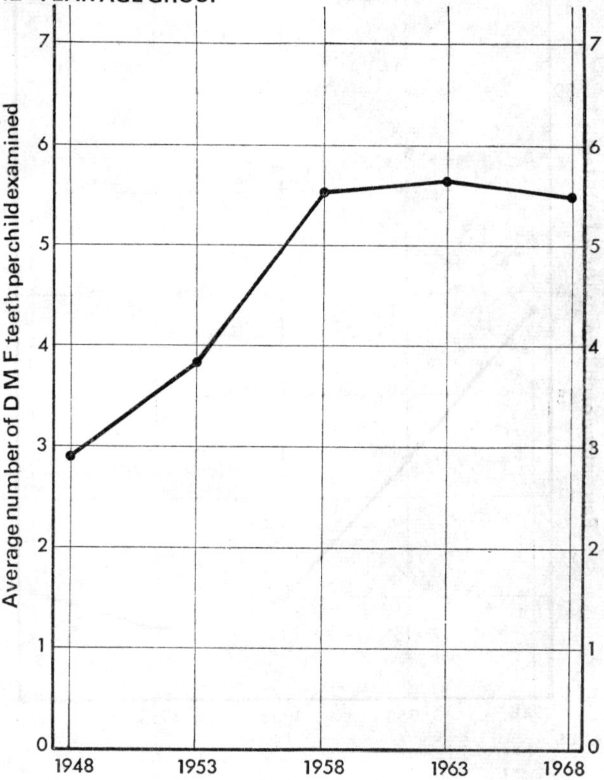

Figure 4.
12–YEAR AGE GROUP

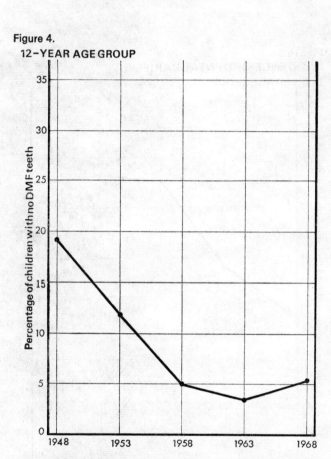

48

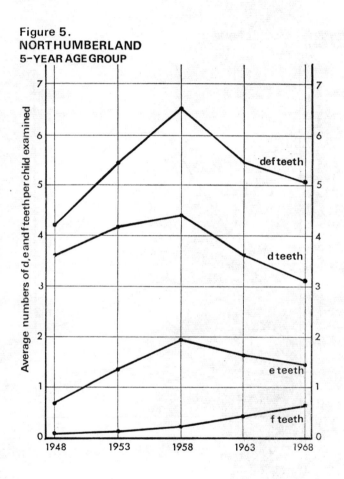

Figure 5.
NORTHUMBERLAND
5-YEAR AGE GROUP

def teeth

d teeth

e teeth

f teeth

Average numbers of d, e and f teeth per child examined

1948   1953   1958   1963   1968

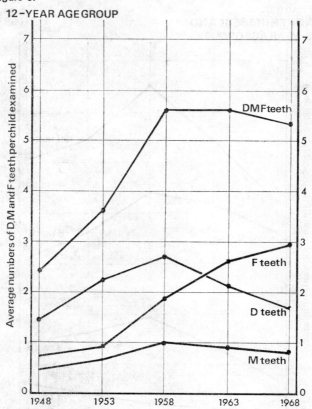

Figure 6.

12-YEAR AGE GROUP

DMFteeth

F teeth

D teeth

M teeth

Average numbers of D,M and F teeth per child examined

50

CHAPTER V

CHILDREN WITH HEARING HANDICAP

The discovery, assessment and education of children with impaired hearing continue to arouse interest and, indeed, controversy and have been the subject of a number of published reports. In 1967, for the first time, children receiving special educational treatment as partially hearing (3,307), outnumbered those being taught as deaf (3,118). Of the partially hearing children about half (1,628) were in 191 special classes in ordinary schools.

Demand for education for young hearing handicapped children has been steadily increasing. Before 1939 only three boarding schools for the deaf had an appreciable number of children under the age of seven which, until 1937, had been the lower limit of compulsory school attendance. In 1937 the lower limit was reduced to five years, but very few children of five years were in special schools by 1939. In January 1967, 565 hearing handicapped children under the age of five years were receiving full-time education in special schools; 499 were being taught as deaf and 66 as partially hearing; 26 children were only two years old of whom 25 were being educated as deaf and one as partially hearing; 7 deaf children and one partially hearing child were in schools for children with more than one handicap. A survey of hearing handicapped children in special classes in ordinary schools showed that out of 828 children in 74 units surveyed, 70 (over 8 per cent) were under the age of five years.

Units for Partially Hearing Children

Units for partially hearing children were the subject of the first of a new series of occasional publications[1]—Education Surveys—prepared by the Department of Education and Science. This survey was carried out jointly by members of H.M. Inspectorate and Medical Officers of the Department and was initiated because of the recent rapid growth of this kind of educational provision. These special classes or units were first started in 1947; development was relatively slow until 1960 since when it has been considerable. At the time of the survey in 1966 there were 162 special classes in England and Wales and they increased to 191 in 1967.

The survey showed that, whereas most of the children admitted to units when they were young were suitable for this kind of provision, in some cases a unit was used for assessment of a child's future educational needs. For children after the infant age it was found to be essential that only those who functioned as partially hearing should be selected for special classes and that they should be seen to have a reasonable prospect of learning to speak, with or without the help of amplification, in a natural way, and more by listening than by lip reading. Doctors who recommended children for special classes without consultation with the teachers concerned were often criticised by these teachers who asserted

---

[1] Units for partially hearing children. Education Survey No. 1. H.M.S.O. 1967.

that without such consultation there was a tendency for children with too many additional handicaps and with an unreasonably great age and ability range to be in the same class. Provided that strict principles of selection were maintained, that preference was given to the needs of very young children and that careful assessment of the progress of each child was made, then children made good progress. It was often found that they did not need the services of specially trained teachers of the deaf after the infant and early junior stage. By this time they had made such progress in development of language that they were able to take their place and hold their own with hearing children in ordinary schools.

The Work of Peripatetic Teachers of the Deaf

Following the survey of special units for partially hearing children, a similar exercise was undertaken to assess the work of peripatetic teachers of the deaf. In 1948 a teacher of the deaf was appointed at the Ear, Nose and Throat Hospital in Golden Square, London, to deal with the educational aspects of hearing handicapped children attending the hospital and who were not in special schools. This was the beginning of the peripatetic teacher service and by January 1968, 148 teachers of the deaf were employed in it. They now have a much wider range of responsibilities than the pioneers who were appointed in 1948. Not only are they expected to help with the diagnosis of hearing handicap in children of all ages, but also to advise parents and teachers in ordinary schools, and to undertake specialised teaching of individual children. This they are often expected to do without having full information about the needs of individual children. To be successful, work of this kind calls for close collaboration with special schools and special classes as well as with ordinary schools so that the full range of educational provision in the neighbourhood is well known and understood by the peripatetic teacher. It is equally necessary that peripatetic teachers should work closely with the doctors (otologists, local authority medical officers and general practitioners) responsible for medical assessment, treatment and supervision and to discuss with them both general policies and the needs of individual children within their families. Close liaison with youth employment officers is also an essential part of the work of peripatetic teachers.

In addition to the 148 trained teachers of the deaf employed as peripatetic teachers by local education authorities and the 173 employed in special classes for hearing handicapped children, 15 were in local education authority audiology clinics, making a total of 336 trained teachers of the deaf employed other than in special schools.

Finger Spelling and Signing

A committee under the chairmanship of Professor M. M. Lewis was appointed by the Secretary of State for Education and Science, in October, 1964, to consider the possible place of finger spelling and signing in the education of deaf children. The report[2] of the committee was presented to the Secretary of State in February, 1968, and published in July of the same year. The committee looked at current arrangements for the education of deaf and partially hearing children and took evidence from a wide circle of witnesses. Although it did not receive any factual evidence that was scientifically valid, there was a considerable weight of informed opinion suggesting that there might be a place for manual media in the education of some deaf children.

---

[2] The Education of Deaf Children: The possible place of Finger Spelling and Signing. H.M.S.O. 1968.

Without exception the witnesses giving evidence to the committee considered that the aim of education for deaf children was to fit them as far as possible for life in a hearing and speaking society, and that for this, knowledge and ability to use language were essential. No organisation or individual presenting evidence suggested that oral methods only were entirely appropriate for all deaf pupils, but some witnesses, experienced in dealing with hearing handicapped children at the present time, felt strongly that oral methods had not yet had a fair trial under ideal conditions. Hearing loss can now be diagnosed at an early age and, if it is followed closely by suitable auditory training that allows a child to compensate for his hearing loss, many children who formerly would have been considered deaf can now be educated as partially hearing. This trend is likely to continue, but there still remain those children who, for one reason or another, make very limited progress in language development when taught by oral methods alone.

The committee in its report recommended a wide range of research studies to decide whether manual media of communication would lead to improvement in the education of deaf children and particularly in the development of language. The committee recognised that each child with a hearing handicap has a unique combination of problems and that there is not such a convenient entity as 'the deaf child'. A wide variety of factors affect the linguistic attainments of children with impaired hearing and this has to be kept in mind when consideration is being given to the use of different media of communication in the education of deaf children.

Discovery of Children with Hearing Handicap

The responsibility of local education authorities for the discovery and management of children with handicaps is clearly defined in the Education Act, 1944, as beginning at the age of 2 years. This is late for beginning auditory training and encouraging language development. Fortunately, most medical officers in the school health service either work in child health clinics themselves or are closely in touch with those who do, so that most babies and young children with a hearing loss severe enough to delay normal language development will be recognised early and known to the principal school medical officer.

In 1967, only 86 of the 162 local education authorities had arranged for the routine audiometric testing of the hearing of all school entrants and two had done so in part of their area; 33 had arranged for the testing of 6 year old, 11 for 7 year old, and 6 for 8 year old children. The remaining 24 did so when thought necessary, for example when teachers, nurses, or school doctors referred children suspected to have defective hearing.

It is desirable that the routine audiometric testing of the hearing of school entrants should be done everywhere. For many children this is the first time that their hearing has been tested since infancy, and for those who may not have had a screening test of hearing in infancy it may well be the first time that their hearing acuity has been measured. Furthermore, for many children the school entrant medical examination at the age of 5 is the first comprehensive medical examination that they have had since infancy; it should be remembered that upper respiratory tract infections involving the middle ear are common in pre-school years and may produce a considerable degree of conductive deafness which may escape notice unless specifically looked for, and may well produce a considerable learning disability.

Advice to Parents

As soon as a child's hearing loss is diagnosed parents need help and guidance, and whoever is to carry out this guidance and counselling should, if possible, be present when the diagnosis is made. Parents need much support, first to accept that their child is handicapped and secondly, to help him to develop his residual abilities. It is important that this help should be available from the very first possible moment. Even if the child is found eventually not to have a severe loss of hearing—and the diagnosis is often difficult to make in a young child, especially if there are other handicaps present—this kind of help and advice is never wasted and can do nothing but good, provided it is not either unduly alarmist or over optimistic and if it is positive and directed towards developing a child's language skills. No harm can be done by positive methods of help directed towards encouraging language in any child, provided that this help correlates with knowledge of the growth patterns in normal child development.

However severely handicapped a child, it is very important that a satisfactory system of communication between him and his parents should be established before he goes to school so that home remains a secure base and his parents continue to be the most important people in his life.

This kind of help to parents is not something to be given on one occasion only, at the time the diagnosis is made. Parents may then be too shocked and distressed to take in all the implications and they may need continuing support for the whole of the child's pre-school and school days as well as after the child has left school.

Assessment

Although the degree of hearing loss may be, in the majority of cases, the most important single handicap governing a child's placement in school, it must be related to other factors and it is necessary to take into account all the evidence which can be obtained. Assessment must be of a total situation and include not only the disability itself, but the child's parents, his social environment, the presence of other handicaps and his personality; other problems, such as mental handicap and defective vision may be complicating factors. Assessment is a team activity involving different disciplines and this is particularly true in sorting out difficult problems.

Doctors, and these may include otologists, paediatricians, neurologists, psychiatrists as well as the school medical officer, teachers, health visitors, social workers and others may well be involved and lines of communication between them are very important and must be kept open. It should be the recognised responsibility of some person to see that all concerned are kept informed of developments and this includes keeping parents informed. The school doctor must accept at least some of this responsibility. Medical information may be of a confidential nature and communication between doctor and doctor is often necessary. There is less likelihood of misunderstandings if medical information is passed in this personal way. The school medical officer is in an ideal position to explain some of the implications of a child's handicap to his parents and it is important that conflicting advice is not given to parents at any stage.

Recommendations for Educational Placement

In 1938 a departmental committee of the then Board of Education reported[3] on the medical, educational and social aspects of the problems of children suffering from defects of hearing not amounting to total deafness. One of their recommendations was that partially deaf children should be educated separately from deaf children. In the Handicapped Pupils and School Health Service Regulations, 1945, a separate category of partially deaf children was defined and, following this, arrangements were made for the separation of the partially deaf from the deaf, especially in boarding schools. A more positive approach to this problems was underlined by the Handicapped Pupils and Special Schools Amending Regulations, 1962, that redefined these children as partially hearing rather than partially deaf.

During these thirty years there have been considerable technical advances in electronics, better methods of medical diagnosis and more understanding of the development of speech and language in normal children. All these emphasise the necessity for more careful assessment of the needs of individual hearing handicapped children than was possible thirty years ago; and school doctors' responsibilities have increased rather than diminished. Thirty years ago there was little choice in the type of education available for hearing handicapped children; if thought to be suitable for education, and fewer of the very severely handicapped were so considered than at the present time, a special school was the only choice available. Now there are special schools, special classes and the possibility of being able to stay in ordinary school provided that auditory training with good amplification has led to the development of language skills at a level which will enable a child to make progress in an ordinary school environment. Parents know of these alternatives and their wishes must be given full consideration before a recommendation is made for the school placement of their child. Sometimes parents' wishes are not in the best educational interests of their child and the handling of such a situation requires wisdom as well as professional knowledge.

To be able to give really helpful advice about suitable educational placement of individual children, school doctors should be knowledgeable about language development and should be able to assess this development without relying only on a child's superficial facility with words in a known and limited context. They should understand the educational implications of a severe hearing handicap and they should appreciate the work of teachers of the deaf. Both doctors and teachers sometimes give parents very firm, usually over-optimistic, advice about the kind of education their child should have at too early a stage in the young child's development. This advice is often based on firmly held individual opinions about the merits of different kinds of education. These opinions are sometimes based on out of date information about special schools and special classes as well as about special facilities and arrangements in ordinary schools. Parents, too, may have strongly held but far from firmly based views about the kind of education they want for their children. In general, parents will accept advice, even if this goes against their own wishes, much more readily from someone who has been seen over the years to have a real concern for their child and for his family than from someone they do not know. To be

---

[3] Report of the Committee of Enquiry into Problems Relating to Children with Defective Hearing. H.M.S.O. 1938.

able to give this advice needs a great deal of detailed knowledge, not only of the child, but of the educational facilities currently available; and there is need for skilled judgement in the assessment of all the various factors concerned.

Advising local education authorities about the school placement of handicapped children is one of the most important duties of a school doctor. Before making his recommendation he ought to have taken fully into account the views of teachers, psychologists, and the various medical specialists concerned; and, too, it should always be appreciated that the school recommended may not be a once for all placement. All handicapped children require continuing skilled educational and medical observation to ensure that the best practicable educational arrangements are made for them. This is particularly important with children with hearing handicap about whose education there has been controversy ever since the first school for the deaf in England was opened in 1792.

There is a wide range of provision available and modern methods of diagnosis have made it possible to be more accurate in the assessment of hearing loss. The refinements of diagnostic techniques, however, sometimes tend to over enthusiasm in their pursuit, and the more pressing, indeed urgent, need for developing language in deaf children is lost sight of. Some of this over enthusiasm was observed during the survey of the work of peripatetic teachers of the deaf. No amount of audiometric testing, however skilled and refined, is in the long run going to teach a child language. Sophisticated diagnostic procedures are necessary for research and may help a teacher in teaching a child language, but they are not an end in themselves. Time is not on the side of the child with a severe hearing loss and the school years are far too short for all that has to be accomplished. To waste what amounts in many cases to quite considerable periods of the time of highly skilled and specially trained staff in testing and re-testing the hearing of children without being able, as a result, to add anything positive to their educational programme is not helpful.

Hearing aids

In 1967 the Ministry of Health announced three improvements in the range of hearing aids to be supplied under the National Health Service. First, the Ministry of Health was developing a completely new body-worn aid which would cater for the majority of those with hearing impairment, including many who were not adequately helped by the current models. While this was being developed the Ministry would provide a limited quantity of one of the existing range of Medresco aids substantially modified to produce some of the special characteristics needed by some hearing impaired persons. In addition, it was hoped during 1968 to start distribution of a head-worn aid. Distribution would initially be limited to school children over the age of seven for whom it was found suitable. It is hoped that these developments will, in time, reduce the number of instances where it is necessary for local education authorities to purchase commercial aids, but there are bound to be some children whose needs can only be catered for by special individual arrangements.

For some time the Royal National Institute for the Deaf has run a service for testing hearing aids and their experts have expressed growing concern at the poor condition of aids sent to them by local education authorities. In 1967 it was decided that the R.N.I.D. would initiate a survey for testing aids in schools in a large local education authority's area. Experienced R.N.I.D. staff travelled from school to school in a mobile van specially equipped for testing. The number of aids found not to be working was very high, and, while the majority of faults found were of a type that could be detected visually without expensive equipment, they did require an understanding of hearing aid technology. Many teachers welcomed advice and assistance and many were reported as feeling at a disadvantage as regards knowledge of modern hearing aids and current testing techniques. The number of spare aids was found to be inadequate. It was felt, too, that some reassessment of the methods of issuing, maintaining and using aids in schools was required.

The evidence provided by this investigation has been supported by a comparable investigation carried out by a consultant otologist in charge of three audiology clinics. The hearing aids of 300 children attending these clinics during three months in 1968 were tested and only a minority of the aids were found to be in satisfactory working order.

Larchmoor School

This school, administered by the Royal National Institute for the Deaf, was opened in February, 1966. It is designed for twenty-five children who, in addition to hearing impairment, have emotional and/or psychological difficulties as well. Children are sent to Larchmoor by local education authorities throughout Britain; most had already attended a special school or a unit for partially hearing children but had proved too difficult to cope with. Many of the children so far admitted had been excluded from their previous school because of behaviour problems. These children need special consideration from a medical as well as an educational point of view and the medical care of the children at Larchmoor is of a comprehensive nature.

A local general practitioner visits several times a week and he has a dual role. He carries out the routine and selective medical examinations required by the school health service as well as acting as family doctor. A consultant psychiatrist spends one session each week at the school. He interviews all applicants for admission and their parents. He has regular case conferences with staff, interviews individual pupils in the school and gives support and guidance to the staff in the management of individual children. A visiting otologist visits monthly to inspect and advise on children's otological problems. Dental care is in the hands of a local dental practitioner who has had extensive experience of deaf patients. The matron, an S.R.N. with Health Visitor's Certificate, is responsible for day to day medication and treatment and also for maintaining contact with parents and for the social case work side of the school's work.

From February, 1966 to November, 1968, 41 children, 28 boys and 13 girls, were admitted. Only two had been found unsuitable after trial, one of these being severely sub-normal and the other suffering from a schizoid disorder. Five children, after investigation and treatment, have been able to return to schools for the deaf or partially hearing units. One child was transferred to an E.S.N. school and another to an independent school. The waiting list in November, 1968, was 15, comprising 13 boys and two girls.

Between February 1966 and November, 1968 a total of 34 children were considered for admission, but not added to the waiting list for various reasons. The most frequently recurring reasons were severe subnormality, educational subnormality where this was considered to be the child's major handicap rather than a hearing problem associated with maladjustment, and maladjustment of an insufficiently severe degree to warrant admission to this special school. It is interesting that in the case of three children the problems were resolved by consultation alone and admission, therefore, was not considered necessary. In its early days the school was asked to admit a number of older children, of 14 years and upwards. This militated against success and now the team which assesses priorities for admission is anxious to confine its activities, as far as possible, to children of primary school age since the prognosis for success and return to neighbourhood school or units is more favourable than it is for older children.

CHAPTER VI

VISION OF SCHOOLCHILDREN

Screening Tests of Visual Acuity

Testing is usually carried out by school nurses, sometimes by clerks, and in a very few areas by audiometricians. Use of the Keystone Vision Screener has rapidly increased; over 40 local authorities use this apparatus, some since 1963, in school health service work as well as for testing adults in general health screening campaigns. The Mavis screener is a comparable machine, but with 14 plates built in and adjusted at the turn of a knob instead of the operator having to insert the appropriate testing cards. Both machines can be operated by an unskilled but conscientious operator after only a few hours training; an understanding of the significance of carrying out the routine reliably and an ability to get on well with children are required. The Keystone determines visual acuity for near and distant objects for each eye separately, muscle balance, depth and colour perception. Special test cards are available for entrants, and modifications of Snellen cards for older children and adults. The Mavis investigates distant visual acuity for each eye separately, vertical and lateral heterophoria, i.e. latent squint for distance, binocular distant vision, near visual acuity for each eye separately at 33 cm, vertical and lateral heterophoria for near vision and binocular near vision. Additional tests are included for suitability for certain occupations e.g. weaving.

These machines are expensive, heavy, and unsuitable for some severely handicapped children, most of whom are probably difficult to assess by any method. They have, however, achieved a popularity ascribable to ease of application by a single operator in any surroundings where there is an electricity supply; a well-lit expanse of 20 feet is not required. So far as is known, there have been no reports that significant abnormalities have been missed, but when these machines are used with young children they have the serious disadvantage that too many of those who fail the tests are found not to have a visual defect when subsequently examined by an ophthalmologist. On account of this, the use of these machines with children under seven years of age has been abandoned in some areas; where they continue to be used it would seem that a second screening test by skilled staff using conventional methods is indicated, and an opportunity provided for discussion with the parents before any child is referred to an ophthalmic clinic.

The vision of entrants should be assessed before, or soon after, starting school by patient and expertly trained staff. The School Health Service Group of the Society of Medical Officers of Health held its first short course on the diagnosis and treatment of visual defects in children, in November, 1968, at Guy's Hospital. A demonstration by Dr. Mary Sheridan was included; she showed that with Stycar material,[1] average three-year old children could co-

---

[1] Obtainable from the National Foundation for Educational Research in England and Wales, 79 Wimpole Street, London W.1.

operate at a distance of 10 feet, using selected letters easily identifiable even by illiterate children. Other methods include use of picture charts, with or without matching of miniature toys, animal charts, inverted E or C (Landolt's rings) charts and numbers. A rapid screening test not giving the actual visual acuity was described by Withnell and Wilson;[2] three white cards are used, printed with one, two or three black blocks arranged so that if a child can correctly state the number of blocks at 6 metres, the visual acuity is at least 6/9.

During 1966, 22,095 entrants to schools throughout England and Wales were found to require treatment for defective vision, and in 1967, 23,253 compared with 20,820 in 1965. This increase in reported visual defects in entrants reflects the rising frequency of vision testing of children soon after they first start school rather than increased incidence. In 1966, only 16 local authorities delayed first examinations of entrants' vision beyond their first year in school, 6 postponing this until 6 years of age, 7 until 7 years of age and 3 until 8 years of age; in 1967, 5 delayed to 6 years of age, 6 to 7 years of age and the same 3 to 8 years of age. It is hard to understand why all local education authorities do not arrange for the vision testing of all children during their first year at school.

There were surprising variations in the frequency of vision testing in the different local education authority areas. In 18 areas all school children, and in one area all except six-year olds, were tested annually; in another area, children with spectacles were tested annually, the rest remaining untested from the age of 7 years until the school leavers' examination; in yet another area, children with a defect found previously were tested annually, but the others only at ages 7, 11 and 14 years; a curious arrangement in one area was that all children except those at grammar schools (among whom refractive errors are common) were tested annually. Elsewhere the arrangements varied from the annual testing of primary pupils only to the annual testing of secondary pupils only.

Over a period of four months in 1968, in various districts of London, a commercial firm used a mobile vision screening unit, equipped with the Mavis apparatus, to test the vision of children and adults. Among those who volunteered to be tested were 375 children, aged 15 years and under. Records were not kept of the children who had previously been tested by the school health service, or of those who might have been prescribed spectacles but were not wearing them on the day they were tested, or, indeed, of those who were wearing glasses when tested although the operators were said to have asked the children who had glasses with them to wear them during the tests.

Of the 375 children 68 were found to have minor, and 56 (15 per cent) more significant, abnormalities. Three children, aged 10, 11 and 14 years, had visual acuity of 6/36 or less in both eyes; 19 had a similar loss in one eye. Two children, aged 9 and 11 years, had bilateral visual acuity 6/18 or less; 5 had a similar loss in one eye. Two boys, aged 14 and 15 years, had visual acuity of less than 6/14 in both eyes; 10 had a similar loss in one eye. Five children had visual acuity of less than 6/10 in both eyes, ten in one eye. One fourteen year old girl had no apparent sight in one eye. Seven children were hypermetropic in both eyes and seven in one eye, all but one being 10 years of age or over. Some had a combination of visual disorders, and 28 showed some evidence of muscle imbalance.

---

[2] Brit. Med. J. 19 October, 1968.

These findings emphasise the need for vision screening tests of all school children annually so that the necessary measures are taken promptly to improve the children's working vision. In 1967, 450,940 school children were found with 'errors of refraction' and squint.

Mr. M. J. Gilkes, F.R.C.S., in an address on 'Problems of Refraction,'[3] pointed out the unfortunate use of words such as 'defect' and 'abnormality' in considering the nature of refraction. He agreed that it might well be that the higher degrees of ametropia arose as a result of different mechanisms from those concerned with the determination of emmetropia, but considered that it was a mistake to use the word 'failure' as part of the description of the factors involved. He mentioned that standard textbooks still headed their chapters, 'Errors of Refraction' and that school doctors continued to write about 'defect of vision'. He suggested that these terms should be replaced by 'Refractive Variations' that carried no lay connotation of disease, and in consequence the term 'adjusting' other than 'correcting' lenses was preferable. He considered the term, 'eyestrain', as a problem of semantics: did anyone now believe that it was possible to strain the syes?

Squint

In 1967, 24,157 schoolchildren, including 11,188 entrants, were found to require treatment for squint; in addition, a further 19,097 children, including 9,669 entrants, were placed under observation for this condition, presumably having already been referred previously for treatment, since any child with a suspected squint should be referred to an ophthalmologist without delay. Failure to recognise squint in a pre-school child increases the risk of development of amblyopia by failure of the establishment of binocular vision, or, where it is in operation, by the suppression of the image produced by one eye where double vision is troublesome. Head tilt or abnormal head posture as well as general appearance should lead the observer to suspect squint; the cover test should be carried out routinely, particularly on young children with a family history of squint, or where there has been recent illness such as whooping cough or measles.

Colour Vision

By 1966, routine colour vision testing of boys was carried out in all but 15 local education authority areas; in one area, grammar school boys only were tested; there was no routine testing of girls in 53 areas. The ages at which testing was done ranged from 5 to 15 years. Some doctors now prefer the Keystone Colour Vision screening tests using coloured balls containing numbers instead of the Ishihara books of coloured plates.

Occasionally, a child who was considered to have normal colour vision when tested in school is later found unsuitable for a particular occupation, e.g. in the Services, on specialised testing by other methods but this is a rare occurrence; it does not detract from the value of routine testing at school before a child has expressed his preference for a particular career. It is probable that a colour vision defect in the presence of normal visual acuity will not be associated with eye disease.

[3] Transactions of the Opthalmological Society Volume LXXXVI 1966

A questionnaire was sent to all principal school medical officers early in 1968 enquiring about difficulties in arranging for the prompt refraction of school-children by ophthalmologists. Completed returns were obtained from 134 of the 172 areas.

In 25 areas, refraction was undertaken by ophthalmologists both in school and hospital clinics; in 89 areas, the work was done only in school clinics; 20 education authorities relied solely on the hospital eye service. The services of ophthalmologists who worked in school clinics were either provided free to local education authorities by regional hospital boards, (in 72 areas), or the education authority employed and paid them, (in 53 areas); in some areas, both types of arrangement were in force; sometimes there was a financial arrangement between the local education authority and the local executive council in respect of the ophthalmologists employed by the local education authority.

A limited amount of the refraction of schoolchildren was done in 19 areas by a few school doctors who were specially experienced in this work. In 46 areas, some children were referred to general practitioners and in 42 areas, some were sent direct to ophthalmic opticians. Thus, in most of the 134 areas there was a wide variety of arrangements for the refraction of schoolchildren. About 40 local education authorities reported various difficulties due mainly to the unavailability of ophthalmologists.

In 1967, the British Medical Association prepared a report on the school ophthalmological service superseding an earlier report, published in 1947, that had opposed the employment of non-medical refractionists in school clinics. In 1968, representatives of the Department of Education and Science, the then Ministry of Health and the Ophthalmic Group Committee of the British Medical Association met to discuss the school ophthalmic service. It was agreed that screening tests of schoolchildren could be done by trained auxiliary staff; that standardised tests, such as the Sheridan-Gardiner, not dependent on literacy, should be given to every child during his first term at school, and that teachers should be encouraged to familiarise these young children with the test material to be used—capital letters, E. game etc. All children who failed these tests should be examined by an ophthalmologist who, if no ocular abnormality or pathological condition of the eye was found, could then refer them for refraction to an optician. It was considered that every local education authority should have the services of an ophthalmic surgeon who should be in clinical charge of the school ophthalmic service, working closely with the principal school medical officer who was in adminis-trative charge of the school health service; there was a good case for the employ-ment of opticians in the school health service to work under the general direction of an ophthalmologist. Since so many hospital ophthalmic out-patient depart-ments were crowded with adult, and often elderly, patients, it was thought highly desirable that schoolchildren should, generally, continue to attend school or other special clinics for examination of their eyes, and that pre-school children should also be encouraged to attend them, as, in fact, many do. There should also be more energetic follow-up of children who failed to keep appoint-ments at school eye clinics. Ophthalmic surgeons doubted if the annual returns of local education authorities gave the true incidence of squint in school-children. Instead of giving the number of children suspected of having squint, it would be more useful to all concerned if all children about whom there was doubt were referred to ophthalmologists and only those in whom squint was diagnosed were included in the annual statistical returns; it was necessary, also, to have information about amblyopia.

Visually Handicapped Children

A Committee of Enquiry into the education of visually handicapped children was appointed by the Secretary of State for Education and Science in October, 1968, 'to consider the organisation of education services for the blind and the partially sighted and to make recommendations'. The Chairman is Professor M. D. Vernon, and members include teachers, educationists, an ophthalmologist and a principal school medical officer. Medical problems of ascertainment and supervision will also be considered, as well as the difficult problem of children with multiple handicaps including poor vision, and the lack of recognition of visual difficulty in some children with other severe handicaps, either mental or physical. The last departmental enquiry was in 1934, since when the problems of partially sighted children have changed. The report of the recent Scottish enquiry[4] into ascertainment should be helpful in indicating the type of teamwork involved, by school medical officer, educational psychologist, teacher of the blind or partially sighted, ophthalmologist, paediatrician and, possibly, psychiatrist, in the proper placement of visually handicapped children.

A symposium[5] on Paediatric ophthalmology was held in Birmingham in April, 1968, sponsored by the Royal National Institute for the Blind and the Spastics Society. Ophthalmologists, paediatricians, psychiatrists, psychologists, school medical officers, (including a general practitioner serving a school for additionally handicapped blind children), and teachers took part in a concentrated programme of lectures, discussions, and demonstrations on eye disorders in children and their medical and educational management. This coming together of some of the various professional workers concerned was very valuable and many useful points emerged, particularly in the discussion.

It is not always appreciated that partially sighted children require more frequent ophthalmic supervision than blind children. It is of vital importance that visually handicapped children who require spectacles should wear them consistently; it is disappointing to find many partially sighted children virtually restricted to functioning as blind because an alternative pair of glasses was not provided during the all too frequent periods when their only pair of spectacles was being repaired. Robust frames can be supplied for thick lenses, and an additional bridge bar, in frame number C 253, can reduce the fragility of the spectacles. Plastic lenses are less heavy than glass; an increasing number of children are now being supplied with contact lenses, in some cases improving their effective vision to such an extent that return to ordinary school is advocated. For partially sighted children dependent on spectacles, there should be no difficulty in obtaining a second pair for school use, and many local education authorities have routine arrangements for this additional provision. School medical officers seeing partially sighted children in ordinary schools as well as in special schools and classes should not only carry out physical examinations

---

[4] Ascertainment of Children with Visual Handicaps: Reports of the Working Party appointed by the Secretary of Scotland, Scottish Education Department, 1969.
[5] Proceedings to be published in 1969.

but should also observe the children in the classroom, in academic and practical work, at physical education, and at play to assess how well they are overcoming their visual handicap.

Survey of Blind and Partially Sighted Children

The report[6] of a survey by a medical officer of the Department of Education and Science of 817 blind and 1,374 partially sighted children in special schools and classes was published in December, 1968. The survey covered children born on or after 1st January, 1951, attending the 20 special schools for the blind and 34 special schools and 8 special classes for partially sighted children in England and Wales during 1962 to 1965. Children were studied in 2 groups: Group A, born in 1951 to 1955, and Group B born in 1956 to 1960 after the years of temporarily high prevalence of retrolental fibroplasia; (isolated occurrences of this condition still, unfortunately, arise).

Blind Children

Apart from prematurity associated with retrolental fibroplasia, the aetiology of most eye conditions was unknown, though there was a family history in 15·3 per cent of the children. In Group A, retrolental fibroplasia predominated, with optic atrophy in second place whereas in Group B, optic atrophy was the commonest cause of blindness, with cataract next. There was a wide range of visual acuity but most of the children were thought to be suitably placed in schools for the blind although a few had some useful vision. Mobility was shown to improve with age, particularly in girls, in whom, in both Groups A and B, it was less good than in boys.

Intelligence quotients were obtained for children born in 1951, 1953 and 1955 and were in the ratio of 23:59:18 for dull: average: superior intelligence compared with the standard distribution of approximately 15: 70: 15. Those with tumours of the eye, diseases of the retina and choroid and cataract tended to have greater intellectual ability than those with optic atrophy and retrolental fibroplasia.

Additional handicaps were present in nearly half the children in Group A and in 59% of the boys and 54% of the girls in Group B. In Group A, physical disability was the commonest additional handicap while in Group B, low intelligence accounted for 31·5%. Of the total additional handicaps of the 817 children, 8·9% had evidence of maladjustment, and the teachers interviewed considered that 36% of the children were emotionally disturbed, incicating a need for psychological and psychiatric investigation.

Partially Sighted Children

Special education for these children started in 1908 with sight-saving classes particularly for those with myopia. Cataract has now become the chief cause of admission to special schools and classes in both groups, with myopia in second place in Group A and nystagmus in Group B. The aetiology was unknown in 45·6% but in 34·4% there was a family history of eye disease. Visual acuity ranged from nearly normal to borderline blind, and of the 1,374 children, 49 were considered educationally blind and 36 were thought suitable for ordinary school; 803 children wore glasses but 476 used no visual aids, including 25

---

[6] Blind and Partially Sighted Children Education Survey No. 4. H.M.S.O. 1968.

with myopia and 2 with hypermetropia and astigmatism for whom it would be reasonable to think that glasses might have been helpful.

Intelligence quotients, of a sample group were in the ratio of 22: 67: 11; over 15% of the children with albinism, diseases of the retina and choroid, buphthalmos, uveitis and tumour of the eye were in the gifted range; the highest percentages of dull children were among those with optic atrophy, myopia, nystagmus and cataract.

Additional handicaps were present in 39% of boys and 40% of girls in Group A, and 41% of boys and 44% of girls in Group B. Physical disability was the commonest additional handicap in both groups, closely followed by low intelligence; speech and language difficulty accounted for over 18% of the total handicaps in both groups. Maladjustment accounted for 12·8% of the total handicaps in Group A and 8·3% in Group B. The teachers considered 32% of the children to be emotionally disturbed, indicating a need for psychological and psychiatric help for partially-sighted children also.

Other Surveys

Fraser and Friedmann[7] studied 776 children in schools for the blind in 1963; they carried out an ophthalmic examination on each child supplemented by a questionnaire to parents and previous medical, social and educational reports. Fifty-five children, whose blindness appeared to be of genetic origin, with various members of their families underwent biological and histochemical tests; clinical and biochemical tests were also carried out for any evidence of inborn errors of metabolism, but these proved negative.

A follow-up investigation was started in 1967 of the partially sighted children with dislocated lenses included in the survey by one of the Department's medical officers in 1962–1965; by the end of 1968, two pairs of siblings were identified with homocystinuria, a condition first described in 1962, and characterised by subluxation of the lenses, skeletal abnormalities, vascular changes and, usually, mental subnormality. Thus, it is likely that some of these children will be found in training centres rather than schools, and may be in schools for the educationally subnormal rather than for the partially sighted. The older siblings were a pair of sisters who had attended a school for the partially sighted and had shown progressive mental deterioration; on reaching school leaving age they were transferred to an adult training centre. The younger siblings were a 10 year old boy attending a school for partially sighted children, having started his education at an ordinary primary school, and his 2 year old sister who had not yet been diagnosed as having dislocated lenses; she was being treated with pyridoxine, the alternative to a low methionine diet, and it was hoped that the vascular, orthopaedic and other manifestations would be avoided.

Burns[8] investigated 2,275 children, in 21 special schools for the educationally subnormal and one for the partially sighted in Liverpool, by urine testing for the presence of excess cystine or homocystine. A positive reaction was obtained from nine children and further analysis showed the presence of homocystine in the urine of two boys aged 6 and 11 years. Investigation of their parents and

---

[7] The Causes of Blindness in Childhood. Johns Hopkins. 1967.
[8] Homocystinuria. The Medical Officer. 25th October, 1968, pp. 237–8.

siblings produced another case, the 4 year old brother of the 11 year old attending a school for educationally subnormal children. The 6 year old boy was attending the special school for partially sighted children, and was severely retarded.

It is important to identify these children both to prevent their further deterioration and to give genetic counselling to their parents; the condition is similar to phenylketonuria in that it is hoped that early recognition and treatment will prevent the manifestation of the full effects of the condition.

CHAPTER VII

VISUALLY HANDICAPPED CHILDREN WITH DEFECTIVE HEARING

A questionnaire was sent in December, 1967, to the 174 principal school medical officers in England and Wales asking for information about children, under the age of six years, who in addition to being visually handicapped were also deaf or partially-hearing; 173 replies were received.

At about the same time the Royal National Institute for the Blind and the Deaf-Blind and Rubella Children's Association were asked for the names of children, under the age of six years, known to them who were visually handicapped and deaf or partially-hearing. Most of the children concerned who were known to these two Associations were also known to principal school medical officers. The names of those who were not included in the questionnaires returned by principal school medical officers were referred to them for further enquiry; it transpired that most of these boys and girls were considered to be severely mentally subnormal and had either a visual or hearing handicap but not both.

In all, 215 children (115 boys, 100 girls), under the age of six years, were found to be visually handicapped and were also either deaf or partially-hearing; 46 had been diagnosed as deaf and blind, 49 as deaf and partially-sighted, 30 as partially-hearing and blind, and 90 as partially-hearing and partially-sighted. Table I gives the regional distribution of the 215 children; no children were known to be affected in 84 of the 173 areas.

TABLE I

Region	Diagnosis				Total
	Deaf/ Blind	Deaf/ Pt. Sighted	Pt. Hear-ing/Blind	Pt. Hear-ing/Pt. Sighted	
Northern	1	7	2	6	16
Yorkshire					
East and West Ridings	4	8	3	5	20
North-Western	4	3	5	10	22
North-Midland	1	3	2	4	10
Midland	7	4	1	7	19
Eastern	5	9	2	7	23
South-Eastern	1	1	1	5	8
Southern	5	1	3	11	20
South-Western	2	4	1	8	15
Outer London	5	2	6	15	28
Inner London	10	3	4	8	25
Wales	1	4	—	4	9
Totals	46	49	30	90	215

Ages of the children. Of the 215 boys and girls 26 were under the age of two years, 23 were between two and three years, 40 between three and four years, 54 between four and five years, and 72 between five and six years. Although the enquiry was not related to children whose mothers were known to have had rubella in the early months of pregnancy, the unusually large and widespread outbreak of rubella in 1962 might have accounted, at least in part, for the larger number of affected children between the ages of four and six years (of course, there is, usually, better ascertainment of older handicapped children). *Placement or recommended placement, of the children.* The local education authorities concerned considered that 89 of the 215 boys and girls were suitable, and 91 not suitable, for education at school; 35 were at home and their future placement had not been finally decided at the time of this enquiry—most of them were either too young (23 were under the age of three years, 14 being under two years), or were so severely handicapped, physically and mentally, that they required further investigation and observation before a reasonably accurate assessment of their 'educability' could be made. Table II gives details of the placement of the 215 children.

TABLE II

		Deaf/ Blind	Deaf/Pt. Sighted	Pt. Hear- ing/Blind	Pt. Hear- ing/Pt. Sighted	Total
Special Schools	In	2	19	4	10	35
	Waiting	3	5	1	1	10
	Recommended	2	1	3	16	22
Special Classes or Units	In	5	2	1	6	14
	Waiting	—	—	—	1	1
	Recommended	—	—	—	1	1
Training Centres	In	2	4	3	7	16
	Waiting	1	—	—	1	2
	Recommended	1	4	3	11	19
Subnormality Hospitals	In	19	5	6	3	33
	Waiting	2	—	—	2	4
	Recommended	3	2	5	7	17
Ordinary School or Nursery	In	—	—	—	6	6
	Waiting	—	—	—	—	—
	Recommended	—	—	—	—	—
Placement Uncertain		6	7	4	18	35
Total		46	49	30	90	215

Of the 46 boys and girls who were diagnosed as being both blind and deaf six were at home and their future placement was uncertain; only 12 were in, or recommended for, a special school, class or unit; and 28 were in, or recommended for, a training centre or subnormality hospital.

The degree of partial hearing or partial sight among the others varied from moderate to severe. In one large city six children were classified as deaf and partially-sighted but their visual defect was said to be 'minor'; all six were at a special school for the deaf.

This relatively small group of multiple handicapped children presented difficult educational, medical and social problems; most were mentally retarded to greater or lesser degree: the greater the retardation the more complex the problems they posed, and not least to their families.

There is need for more specialised facilities for them, and for more supportive services for their parents. They require medical and psychological observation and investigation from an early age, and often for a prolonged period, so that well balanced educational and medical assessments of their needs, and recommendations for the most practicable means of providing for them, can be made. Much still has to be learnt about techniques for teaching them. There is no single administrative procedure for dealing adequately with all of them. It is likely that more than half of them will require community care for the whole of their life.

There are, however, good reasons for expecting that a reliable and safe vaccine against rubella will yet be found and so reduce the number of children born with these grievous multiple defects.

CHAPTER VIII

PHYSICALLY HANDICAPPED CHILDREN

The changing pattern of disability

In recent years there has been much comment about changing pattern of the handicaps which are found in the children who are admitted to schools for the physically handicapped throughout England and Wales.

A review of developments in this field was published in 1958[1] which indicated that even then more attention was being paid to children handicapped by spina bifida and how improvements in operative techniques were allowing the children, who previously would have been severely disabled by gross limb deformities plus double incontinence, to become more social acceptable and with attention to bowel and bladder training, to be admitted in increasing numbers to the schools for the physically handicapped.

A quarter of a century of so ago tuberculosis, poliomyelitis, heart disease and congenital defects were the commonest causes of disability among physically handicapped school children. In 1964, a survey[2] of children in the special schools showed that cerebral palsy, poliomyelitis, heart disease, congenital deformities and spina bifida were the chief causes of disability and indicated clearly a change in the relative importance of the various disabilities.

The numbers on the registers of special schools for delicate and physically handicapped pupils in England and Wales, as at 18th January, 1968, are summarised in Table I.

---

[1] Health of School Child 1956/7. H.M.S.O. 1958.
[2] Health of School Child 1964/5. H.M.S.O. 1966.

TABLE I

Number of Physically Handicapped and Delicate Children in Special Schools

Main Disability		Boys	Girls	Total for Disability
Cerebral Palsy	(i) (ii)	999 515	792 459	2,765
Spina Bifida	(i) (ii)	381 112	426 127	1,046
Muscular Dystrophy ..	(i) (ii)	228 207	34 36	505
Haemophilia	(i) (ii)	97 80	— —	177
Post Poliomyelitis.. ..	(i) (ii)	94 129	86 133	442
Heart Disease—Congenital and Rheumatic ..	(i) (ii)	246 127	219 116	708
Congenital Deformities of Limbs	(i) (ii)	181 62	146 53	442
Perthe's Disease	(i) (ii)	97 8	23 6	134
Other Physical Handicaps and Delicate	(i) (ii)	4,051 2,375	2,660 1,572	10,658
Total on School Registers	(i) (ii)	6,374 3,615	4,386 2,502	16,877

Note: in 2nd column (i)=pupils 11 years of age and under
(ii)=pupils 12 years of age and over.

There were also, in January 1968, 309 physically handicapped pupils in 35 special classes in ordinary schools. In the 12 classes for 141 'delicate' pupils there might also have been some children who could have been considered to be physically handicapped as the 'delicate' category is widely and differently interpreted. A number of the children who were disabled as a result of poliomyelitis contracted the disease overseas. Hidden among the statistics are the depressing numbers of children who were needlessly injured as a result of road, or other, accidents. The relatively high incidence of congenital deformity of limbs is due to the fact that the children with severe limb deformities which might have been attributable to the drug thalidomide are now all of compulsory school age. More than half these children are attending ordinary primary schools. They have integrated well, and are able to take a full part in school life and activities if they have sympathetic, but not over-protective, handling by their teachers; they receive much help from the schools' medical and educational advisers, and guidance on the use of prostheses and other aids from the various children's prosthetic units and artificial limb and appliance centres which they attend periodically. It would be unrealistic, however, not to admit that there still remain some children whose problems have not yet been resolved satisfactorily, and there is, therefore, need for regular review of their progress as well as continued support for their families by the social workers and other professional staff concerned.

71

Spina Bifida

Incidence

The reported incidence of spina bifida has varied from area to area for a wide variety of reasons: among those which have been suggested are a true regional variation, genetic factors, and seasonal incidence. The Registrar General has depended on the voluntary notification of cases and there are thought to have been local variations in the methods of ascertainment and the type of case notified. An incidence rate of 1·73 per 1,000 live births has been suggested as a present estimate. This is based on the Registrar General's figures that are at present available and which suggest that about 40% of the children will survive to the age of 5 years.

Some problems of spina bifida

In spina bifida some of the vertebrae, or spinal bones, which normally cover and protect the spinal cord, fail to develop properly, and the spinous process is divided or bifid. The term spina bifida covers a number of conditions which are usually associated with abnormalities of the spine, the spinal cord, or the central nervous system. Two types only need to be considered here. In the meningocele type the protrusion or lump on the back, is always covered with skin and contains no nerve tissue; it rarely gives rise to trouble, and the results of operation are excellent. Unfortunately, the majority are meningomyeloceles in which there is a protrusion of the cord and nervous tissue into a cystic swelling or open wound. In this type, which is also known as spina bifida cystica, the spinal cord is in the shape of a flat plate and the neural plaque is exposed on the surface or there is a thin walled sac which is covered only with a thin membrane. Since the spinal cord and associated nerve roots are involved there is a loss of sensation and flaccid paralysis of the lower limbs, with loss of sphincter control. The degree of paralysis varies with the size and situation of the lesion and from one child to another. A high incidence of hydrocephalus, or abnormally rapid enlargement of the head, is associated with meningomyelocele which occurs most commonly in the lower dorsal and lumbar regions of the spine. It is important to remember that the upper extremities and upper trunk develop normally and this will help the child to achieve mobility and independence in daily living activities.

The Complications of Meningomyelocele

The complications of meningomyelocele and the dramatic suddenness with which they may occur, combined with the fact that it is only within the last decade or so that an appreciable number of babies survive meningitis, other infections or ever increasing hydrocephalus which used to kill nearly all affected babies, reinforce the recommendation that these children should all be under the supervision of trained and experienced staff. Those who have had a decompression valve fitted, especially if under five years of age, are particularly at risk medically and school nurses must therefore be able to detect the first signs of trouble.

The surgical repair and covering of the meningomyelocele, and the decision about the need to control the hydrocephalus which occurs in about 80% of cases by a 'shunting' operation, such as ventriculo-cardiac drainage, will have been taken soon after the birth. When the child is admitted to school ventriculo-cardiac drainage will already have been established but will require intelligent observation, as acute hydrocephalus is a serious neurological emergency. Failure to relieve the pressure on the brain may reduce the intellectual capacity permanently.

At operation a narrow tube is inserted into the cavity of the brain and is led outside the skull beneath the skin, down behind the ear into the jugular vein. In this way the cerebro-spinal fluid passes from the brain cavity to the heart and circulates with the blood in the normal way. A one-way valve to prevent back flow, usually of the Holter type, is situated in the tube behind the child's ear and may easily be felt. The school nurse, or the parents, can be taught how to press on the valve to release any temporary block, but too much handling may be harmful.

Abnormalities in the urinary system are relatively frequent. Each child should have had an early thorough urological examination and then may probably require further examinations at yearly intervals. Where the meningo-myelocele is situated in the lumbar or sacral region, the sphincters of the bladder are usually involved resulting in a constant leakage as the bladder fills and the urine overflows. A residue of urine remains in the bladder which never completely empties. In infancy and early childhood regular manual expression by the mother or nurse will ensure that the bladder is emptied periodically. Later on the children learn to do this for themselves. Frequent testing and bacteriological examination of the urine are necessary in order to control infection and indicate the need for treatment with antibiotics, which may have to be continued for a considerable time. A urinary tract infection may be indicated by a listless, apathetic child who has a raised temperature. Permanent damage to the kidneys, with perhaps hypertension, may result from a combination of infection and obstruction. The onset of renal failure may be slow but progressive, so that it is a very real threat to life in older children.

If the incontinence of urine continues, or if it is considered necessary in order to prevent progressive renal damage, a urinary diversion operation may be advised. The ureters, which lead from the kidneys to the bladder, are detached from the bladder and inserted into a section of the small intestine (ileum), one end of which is brought out through the skin of the abdomen to form an opening or 'spout' over which a rubber bag is fitted. Hence the urine drains from the kidneys into the rubber bag and the child may achieve a great measure of independence. Normal control may sometimes be achieved, even in an apparently unlikely case, and so the operation is usually delayed until the child is of primary school age; this operation is seldom necessary for boys, whose incontinence can be helped by the use of a suitably designed urinal fitted over the penis. Attention must be paid to the proper cleaning and storage of bags and urinals; disposable bags may prove to be satisfactory.

Children with spina bifida are also particularly liable to develop chest infections, especially pneumonia.

Bowel training should be started early, for while is is acceptable for a baby or toddler to wear napkins, it is an embarrassment for a school child. Most of the children cannot produce a bowel action without some assistance. The aim should be to achieve a regular morning action. This may need much patience and encouragement as well as the use of mild laxatives or suppositories, or perhaps even an occasional enema. Schools which accept children with meningomyelocele will need more than the usually accepted number of water-closets, most of which should be suitably positioned for wheelchair users and all of which should afford privacy for the children. There can be no excuse for the routine seen recently at a well-known residential school for the physically handicapped where every morning about 20 children with spina bifida were lifted up onto various trolleys and tables and manual removal of faeces was performed by the nurse and young untrained child care staff with no attempt at privacy, or bowel training. It has rightly been said that 'the rewards of a happy and socially adjusted child far outweigh the effort involved'.[3]

The importance of mobility cannot be overstressed. Early physiotherapy is essential for the majority of children with spina bifida, where the aim is to achieve independence of mobility either unaided or with the end of a walking-appliance or caliper. The non-handicapped child learns to stand and walk sometime before his second birthday and the same principle should apply to the physically handicapped. Possibly more than half the children with meningo-myelocle will have a partial paralysis and some a severe paralysis of the lower limbs. Others may be born with a congenital limb deformity such as congenitally dislocated hips. In a series of cases referred for orthopaedic treatment during the past 10 years Mr. E. H. Strach[4] found that 46% had dislocation of the hip. Orthopaedic surgeons now operate to correct dislocated hips as early as the age of 2 years to help the children to become ambulant. Unequal pull of the muscles, the stronger muscles pulling the others out of shape, or faulty posture, may cause secondary deformities later. It has recently been recognised that children who have to be confined to a wheel chair for considerable periods may need to restrict their diet to prevent the additional handicap of obesity.

Trophic skin ulceration is common, as many of these children are anaesthetic from the waist down and nearly always have impaired circulation. The ulcers may be due to lack of sensation, injury or infection and may prove very difficult to heal. At Coney Hill School children are encouraged to look at their pressure points in strategically placed mirrors. They also carry with them a piece of protective foam rubber. Children with spina bifida are particularly vulnerable to cold classrooms and sanitary annexes, and to burns or scalds from unguarded hot water pipes, radiators or overwarm bath water. The most usual sites for trophic ulcers are the buttock, sacral areas or where there is pressure from calipers.

Fractures of bones usually involving the femur, tibia and fibula are a relatively common occurrence,[5] the child being quite unaware of what has happened because of lack of feeling, or anaesthesia, in the area. These fractured bones break and heal easily and the fractures may be multiple.

Some Educational Aspects

There is at present no clear indication of the degree of educability of children who are handicapped by spina bifida, but it would seem safe to assume that early operation followed by intensive medical care throughout their first few years, will not only increase their life expectancy but will allow them to grow up to be more physically independent and mentally able as citizens than was generally the case about 10 years ago.

[3] Swinvard, C. A. (1964). The child with Spina Bifida. Association for the aid of Crippled Children, New York.
[4] Strach, E. H., Brit. Med. J., 23rd September, 1967.
[5] Quibell, E. P. Proc. Rog. Soc. Med. Vol. 60. August 1967.

The Report of the Joint Sub-Committee of the Standing Medical Advisory Committee[6] suggested that, where closure had been undertaken within the first 24 hours of life, nearly three-quarters of the babies with spina bifida cystica will survive and will make a partial or complete recovery. Of the survivors about one-third will have normal, or only slightly paralysed lower limbs not requiring orthopaedic treatment. One-third will have congenital limb deformities and paralysis but with orthopaedic treatment they should be able to walk without, or with minimal, splintage and attend schools for the physically handicapped. The remaining one-third will be severely paralysed, some becoming ambulant with the aid of splints and some requiring the help of a wheelchair.

In several areas, notably Sheffield, Liverpool and five of the southern counties, studies have been carried out to try to form some estimate of educability.[7] A follow-up of babies treated for spina bifida at the Sheffield Children's Hospital neonatal surgical unit during the five years from 1959–1964 indicated that out of every 100 babies treated, 70 lived, of whom 55 had normal mental development, 10 were considered to be educationally subnormal and five unsuitable for education at school.

In 1967[8] all local education authorities were asked, when considering their school building programmes, to review the likely future demand for places for children with spina bifida; and again in 1968,[9] the Department of Education and Science indicated that building programmes which would increase the number of places available for children handicapped by spina bifida would be given priority.

The first special school for children with spina bifida was opened in 1959 at Coney Hill, Kent by the Shaftesbury Society, and a residential nursery school for 21 children was opened in September 1967 in the same grounds. The need for physically handicapped children to start their education early has long been recognised so that they may explore their environment and have the stimulus of other children. Education in this context also includes training in the management of incontinence and help from physiotherapists and others to achieve the early ambulation which is so important. It is also recognised that wherever practicable young children should be at home; at Coney Hill every effort is made to keep close liaison with the homes. Rooms for parent training have been included at the new nursery unit; there is also close liaison with the paediatric surgical unit. The resident staffing of the nursery unit consists of a fully qualified sister-in-charge with three full-time nurse assistants for each of the three groups of children in the nursery school; there is also one trained nursery teacher with two assistants and a physiotherapist. The domestic staff consists of a cook and an assistant as well as one domestic help who also assists with the children's meals. The headmaster and resident matron of Coney Hill School exercise overall supervision.

A second special (day) school for children with spina bifida, which is due to open early in 1969 in Sheffield for 55 children, also has a nursery class; and a third school is planned for Liverpool for 80 day and 50 boarding children.

---

[6] 'Surgery for the Newborn'. Rpt. Jnt. Sub.Cmtt. of Stand. Med. Adv. Cmtts. H.M.S.O. 1968.
[7] Health of School Child 1962/3. H.M.S.O., 1964.
[8] Circular 10/67. Department of Education and Science. July 1967.
[9] Circular 20/68. Department of Education and Science. October 1968.

There are about 140 day, and 40 residential special schools that accept incontinent children and consideration is being given to the suitability of their premises and staffing for the increasing number of children with spina bifida who are already requiring placement. In many cases increased sanitary accommodation, with provision for wheelchair users and for dealing with incontinence in privacy, plus the appointment of sufficient welfare assistants are all that are required. In other older buildings quite drastic alterations may be necessary. It is appreciated that there must be a limit to the number of incontinent children admitted to any one school and many schools are reported to have already reached this limit.

Haemophilia

Haemophilia is the best known of the illnesses related to blood coagulation. It is an hereditary disease affecting boys, which causes excessive bleeding and haemorrhages, either internally or into the joints where it may lead to permanent disability in severe cases between the ages of 3 to 14 years.

Two types of haemophilia may be distinguished, one where there is a deficiency of Factor viii and another where there is a deficiency of Factor ix (Christmas disease).

Whether a boy attends a special school or an ordinary school is of less importance than the availability of a hospital where effective treatment may be given immediately. This may entail special arrangements for rapid transport and there should be an awareness on the part of the school staff that joint haemorrhages are extremely painful. The boy with severe haemophilia can usually indicate accurately that a haemorrhage has taken place without the need for extensive examination; he should be allowed to sit quietly until transport is available.

The aim of treatment is to replace the missing clotting factors as soon as possible after the onset of the bleeding. The use of cryoprecipitate has given encouraging results especially in young haemophiliacs and there is now a possibility that prophylactic therapy may develop with cryoprecipitate when the present difficulties of supply have been overcome.

There are at present 15 Haemophilia Diagnostic and Registration Centres throughout England and Wales, where diagnosis and advice are available, and three Special Treatment Centres at Oxford, Manchester and Sheffield.

Cerebral Palsy

Cerebral palsy still accounts for the largest number of phsycally handicapped children in special schools. In 1968 there were 2,765 such children and educational provision has greatly increased over the past 20 years or so.

Cerebral palsy cannot be regarded as a specific disability but rather as a complex of multiple handicaps, for the spastic child may also be physically handicapped, mentally retarded, emotionally disturbed, deaf or partially hearing, or have defects of vision or speech. Many present teaching problems needing the help of teachers with special experience, and small classes, with the help of a full medical team as well as regular physiotherapy, speech therapy or help from a teacher of the deaf or educational psychologist. Many severely handicapped children are in the special schools for cerebral palsied children

76

"Home Economics Class, St. Patrick's School for delicate girls, Hayling Island, Hampshire."

"Girls at Work in the Senior Classroom, St. Patrick's School for delicate girls, Hayling Island, Hampshire"

A Music Lesson at St. Patrick's School for delicate girls, Hayling Island, Hampshire.

Physically handicapped boys and girls playing with an old tractor at the Inner London Education Authority's school for the physically handicapped, Staplefield Place, Handcross, Sussex.

Physically handicapped boys playing with an old Tiger Moth plane and an old Brighton trolley bus at the Inner London Education Authority's school for the physically handicapped, Staplefield Place, Handcross, Sussex

Larchmoor School for maladjusted deaf or partially hearing children, run by the Royal National Institute for the Deaf, at Stoke Poges, Buckinghamshire.

6th Form Girls at Florence Treloar School for physically handicapped, Holybourne, Near Alton, Hampshire.

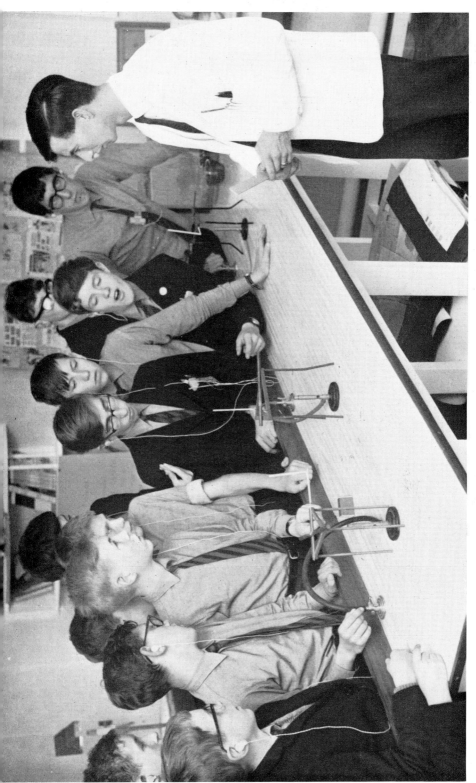

Partially hearing boys at a lesson on the expansion of metal, Ovingdean Hall School for the partially hearing, Brighton.

(*photo by courtesy of Evening Argus, Brighton*)

Painting activities of infants, Ovingdean Hall School for the partially hearing, Brighton.

only which are run by the Spastic Society. Others are suitably placed in the day or residential special schools accepting the full range of physically handicapped pupils. In all these schools physiotherapy is now available.

Education, including educational assessment, at the nursery stage is particularly valuable for the child with cerebral palsy, along with early physiotherapy and early orthopaedic treatment. It is vital to provide help during the pre-school period or 'sensitive' time for the acquisition of speech and language upon which a child's intellect, personality and emotional adjustment depends.

The fact that cerebral palsy still constitutes the chief group of physically handicapped children is not without significance. Among the children with cerebral palsy included in a survey[10] of special schools in 1964, about 40% were considered by their teachers to be educationally subnormal, 10–20% had defective hearing and many others had defects of vision, speech and language. This has, hitherto, caused some parents, and doctors, to think that the special schools for the physically handicapped cater only for the educationally backward. It is likely that this situation will change substantially in the next few years when the largest group of pupils in special schools for the physically handicapped may be those with spina bifida; this change is already becoming apparent in the special schools.

Physically Handicapped Children in Ordinary Schools

It was stated in 1954 that 'no handicapped pupil should be sent to a special school who can be satisfactorily educated in an ordinary school. Where a special school is necessary a day school is preferable if it offers a satisfactory and practicable solution'.[11] Since they must eventually live in the ordinary community physically handicapped children ought, if possible, to attend selected ordinary day schools; this may not always be practicable for educational, social, or geographical reasons but the parents' wishes and the child's personality must always be considered. It is fundamental that children handicapped by spina bifida should attend schools as near their homes as possible, but they should also be within reasonable travelling distance from the hospital responsible for their treatment and supervision.

Children Born in Wales with Spina Bifida

One of the Department's medical officers studied the incidence of spina bifida in North and South Wales in 1965 to 1968 and inquired into the degree of handicap in those who survived; she also reviewed the special educational provision made, or planned, for them. The following is a report of her findings.

Between 1965 and 1968 the number of babies born with spina bifida and notified rose from 17 to 33 in North Wales and fell from 176 to 109 in South Wales. Figure 1 gives the information for each of the four years.

---

[10] Henderson, P. Brit. med. J., 1968, 2, 329–336.
[11] Circular 276. Department of Education and Science, June 1954.

FIGURE 1

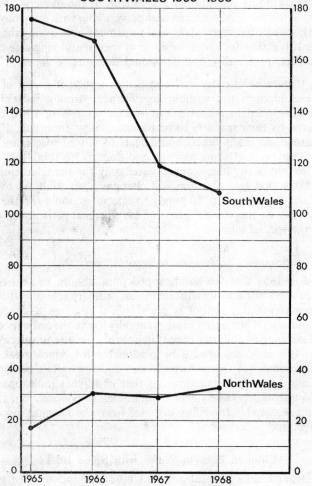

Figure 1.
TOTAL CASES OF SPINA BIFIDA BORN IN NORTH AND
SOUTH WALES 1965–1968

The incidence per 1,000 total births is shown in Table 1

TABLE I

Incidence of Spina Bifida /1,000 total births

Region	1965	1966	1967	1968
N. Wales..	1·70	3·18	3·00	3·32
S. Wales ..	4·73	4·39	3·42	3·12

Tables II and III give the numbers of still births, live births, deaths and survivors for the three years 1965 to 1967 in North and South Wales

TABLE II

North Wales 1965–67

	1965	1966	1967
Still Births ..	5	11	8
Live Births ..	12	20	21
Deaths ..	4	7	6
Survivors ..	8	13	15
Total Births	17	31	29

TABLE III

South Wales, 1965–67

	1965	1966	1967
Still Births ..	45	53	23
Live Births ..	131	105	96
Deaths ..	64	58	40
Survivors ..	67	47	56
Total Births	176	158	119

Table IV gives the still births, deaths and survivors as percentages of the total births for North and South Wales separately.

TABLE IV

Stillbirths, deaths and survivors expressed as percentages of total spina bifida births

Region	Category	1965	1966	1967	1968
N. Wales ..	% SBs.	29·4	35·5	27·6	27·3
	% Deaths	23·5	22·6	20·7	30·3
	% Survivors	47·1	41·9	51·7	42·4
S. Wales ..	% SBs.	25·6	33·5	19·3	16·5
	% Deaths	36·4	36·7	33·6	32·1
	% Survivors	38·1	29·7	47·1	51·4

The Medical Officers of Health of the counties and county boroughs in Wales provided not only information about still births, live births and the survival of infants suffering from spina bifida, but, where possible, they also gave an opinion on the degree of handicap and the anticipated educational and social needs of individual children. The clinicians concerned, the Welsh Hospital Board and the Department of Child Health of the Welsh National School of Medicine were helpful in giving access to hospital records; this not

79

only expanded the available information, but also provided a cross-reference of the treated survivors. Also of value was the birth register of congenital abnormalities compiled in the Department of Social Medicine at the Welsh National School of Medicine for parts of South Wales involving two of the review years.

Not all medical officers of health appeared to have been informed of all infants suffering from this defect in their own areas. Unless they are given full information about these children they cannot adequately advise their education authority on special education provision for them.

In attempting to make deductions from an examination of the returns, certain points should be kept in mind. The term 'survival' means that the infant was still alive at the time of collection of the initial data (June–November, 1968). It is essential that all babies born with spina bifida should be kept under continuing review and their records kept up to date. Predictions of the possible ultimate degree of handicap in an infant who may be anything from one to three years old must, of necessity, be imperfect. In this context, 'minimal handicap' can be defined as likelihood that the child will be able to attend an ordinary school; 'moderate handicap' indicates that the child will possibly need considerable support, either in a residential or day special school, or in a special unit within an ordinary school; and 'maximum handicap' covers those infants needing special care who appear to be grossly handicapped, physically and mentally.

Tables V and VI give for North and South Wales separately the numbers, and percentages, of children with minimal, moderate and maximum handicaps, born in 1965 to 1967, who had survived up to the time of this survey in June to November, 1968.

TABLE V

N. Wales (actual numbers in backets)

	1965	1966	1967
Minimal handicap..	12·5% (1)	15·3% (2)	20·0% (3)
Moderate physical handicap	62·5% (5)	61·4% (8)	53·3% (8)
Maximal handicap	25·0% (2)	23·1% (3)	26·7% (4)

TABLE VI

S. Wales (actual numbers in brackets)

	1965	1966	1967
Minimal handicap..	43·3% (29)	44·7% (21)	32·1% (18)
Moderate physical handicap	44·8% (30)	40·4% (19)	51·8% (29)
Maximal handicap	6·0% (4)	4·3% (2)	8·9% (5)
Not yet classified ..	6·0% (4)	10·7% (5)	7·1% (4)

80

As mentioned earlier, the original aim of the review was to make an approximate estimate of the future educational and social needs of the children with spina bifida in Wales. In the north of the Principality, with a population of approximately half a million people, there would seem to be at present a need to provide special educational facilities for up to eight children a year.

In South Wales the picture is perhaps less clear, but some facts would seem to have been established. The reported incidence of spina bifida has been decreasing since 1965; the survival rate is now in the region of 50%, due, most probably, to the opening of the Spina Bifida Unit at Cardiff Royal Infimary and the co-ordination of the various clinical specialities involved in the treatment of the condition; over 50% of the survivors will need some form of special educational treatment. In South Wales, on present evidence, it seems likely that 25% of all spina bifida births in any year, or 50% of all those who survive infancy, may require special provision.

In Cardiff, the next stage in the care of these children has recently been met by the provision of developmental assessment facilities in a nursery class environment at the Preswylfa Nursery School for Handicapped Children. In this unit multiply handicapped children over the age of two years are to be admitted for education, training, remedial treatment, and for ascertainment of their ultimate educational needs. The full staff of the unit will comprise medical officer, nursery teachers, nursery nurses, physiotherapist, psychologist, speech therapist and any other therapist who may be required.

Even with this unit there will still be a considerable load on the special residential schools for physically handicapped children, and some extension of them may be necessary.

The special school for physically handicapped pupils in North Wales, Ysgol Gogarth, is to be enlarged by a further 40 beds in the 1970–71 building programme. This will give an opportunity to improve the existing facilities within a school which was not originally designed to provide for children with spina bifida. Alterations in the pattern of diseases, and changes in methods of treatment inevitably hamper the efficiency of such schools. It may be that changing attitudes towards prolonged hospitalisation may lead to shortened periods of stay for active treatment, so that children may be transferred back from hospital to their residential school for nursing care in their familiar educational environment.

South Wales, with a numerically larger problem, will require a regional service in the near future. At a recent meeting of the Welsh Joint Education Committee it was decided that an additional school was necessary for physically handicapped children in South Wales, in addition to special day units and special nursery classes, which may be set up by the authorities to meet their individual needs.

Clearly, periodic re-assessment of the needs of these children will be necessary and with the help and co-operation of the principal school medical officers throughout Wales machinery has now been established to make this possible.

It is essential to have a framework of services for this group of children, beginning with the diagnostic facilities and paediatric surgery which are initially necessary. Whilst progress has been made in the clinical treatment available for these children, the supportive counselling service within the community has lagged behind. There is, however, an increasing awareness of the need to advise, support, and help the parents of very young handicapped children and health visitors and social workers are becoming more and more involved in caring for this group of children.

In short, provision for children with spina bifida must include: diagnosis and surgical treatment in early infancy; continuing medical supervision, treatment and support in a paediatric assessment centre and suitable educational and medical provision from the age of 2 or 3 years.

CHAPTER IX

CHILDREN WHO HAVE DIFFICULTY IN LEARNING

The term 'educationally subnormal' was first introduced in the Handicapped Pupils and School Health Service Regulations, 1945. There has been increasing criticism of the term but, as yet, there is no unanimity as to what should replace it. The Plowden Report[1] commented on the unnecessary distress it caused parents and recommended that it should be replaced by 'slow learners'. This was also the term used in the Gittens Report.[2] In 1964, the then Ministry of Education published a pamphlet (Number 46) on the needs of educationally subnormal children and on ways these could be met. The pamphlet had the title 'Slow Learners at School'. It stated: 'Educational backwardness is not regarded as a single, sharply defined characteristic as was 'mental deficiency' but rather as a matter of degree and origin, and caused by a combination of circumstances. No attempt is made to define, classify or categorise backward children, nor is special education looked upon as a form of education peculiar to special schools.'

In practice, however, the use of the term 'educationally subnormal' is too often restricted to children who are considered to need full-time education in a special school principally because of educational backwardness associated with a lower than average I.Q. It must be again emphasised that this was not the intention of the Handicapped Pupils and School Health Service Regulations, 1945, nor of the Handicapped Pupils and Special Schools Regulations, 1959. Educationally subnormal pupils include both children who are educationally backward (i.e.—their attainments are appreciably less than those of the average child of the same age), whether or not they are mentally retarded, and also children of average and above average ability who, for various reasons, are educationally retarded (i.e.—their attainments are not commensurate with their ability); they also include both children who require 'some specialised form of education wholly . . .' and those who require it '. . . partially in substitution for the education normally given in ordinary schools'.

Diagnosis

Children who are failing in school are mostly referred by their teachers for medical examination either because of their poor progress or their behaviour, or both. Educational backwardness and disturbed behaviour should first be viewed by school doctors as symptoms requiring diagnosis. The fact that a child is so backward in class that his teacher has asked for an examination more than likely means that the child is needing more help than is normally

---

[1] Children and Their Primary Schools. A Report of the Central Advisory Council for Education (England), 1967. Vol. I. H.M.S.O.
[2] Primary Education in Wales. A Report of the Central Advisory Council for Education (Wales), 1967. H.M.S.O.

83

available in an ordinary school, i.e. he is educationally subnormal. What is required of the school doctor is a diagnosis of the cause of the backwardness, in the light of which he can advise both the teacher and the local education authority.

It may be that the doctor's assessment of the case will lead him to advise that the child's learning difficulties may best be met by the regime and teaching skills that are only available through whole-time attendance at a special school.

Alternatively, it may be that the disorder underlying the educational backwardness will be found to be one affecting the child's hearing or his emotional development and social adjustment, uncomplicated by intellectual retardation. Treatment of the underlying condition, with supporting advice for the teacher, may enable the child to overcome his learning difficulties.

Often, however, the educational backwardness is found to be associated with less than average intelligence but not so low that the child is considered to require education in a special school for the educationally subnormal. The teacher may then be told only that the child is not, therefore, educationally subnormal; the child returns to his school and no recommendation is made for special education and no advice is given the teacher. This sequence of events should not arise if the school doctor concentrates on making a diagnosis of the cause of the child's educational backwardness and an assessment of his needs rather than on the question of whether or not the child should be ascertained as educationally subnormal. These children are the concern not only of the school health service but also of the school psychological service, and it is essential that both services should work in close partnership; unfortunately, there is a continuing shortage of educational psychologists.

Formal and informal ascertainment

Circular 11/61, issued by the then Ministry of Education in July, 1961, reviewed some of the ways in which special education could be arranged for educationally subnormal pupils. The Circular drew attention to the fact that whilst local education authorities had the duty to ascertain which children required special educational treatment all the formal procedures set out in Section 34 of the Education Act, 1944 need not be followed if a parent agreed to his child being admitted to a special school.

The Circular welcomed the fact that some local education authorities were already using informal ascertainment procedures but advised that a medical examination would, nevertheless, normally be desirable to ensure that physical disorders that might contribute to the child's backwardness were not overlooked. This advice has sometimes been forgotten, or ignored, and children have been admitted to special schools and special classes without this precaution.

Some factors which contribute to difficulties in learning

Every child who has difficulty in school requires physical (including neurological) and psychological examination to discover defects of vision, hearing, movement or speech, or disturbance in emotional or intellectual development that may be a primary or contributory cause of his difficulties. The influence of social factors also needs to be considered. Frequently, a number of disorders contribute to his poor performance in school.

Physical examination

A general physical examination may bring to light impairment of vision or hearing that may be alleviated, or chronic ill-health that may be treated. General malaise may reduce a child's interest in learning and class activities, and recurrent minor illness may cause repeated absence from school, which has been found to be educationally more harmful than an occasional long period of absence.[3]

It has long been thought that educationally subnormal children have more than their share of physical defects and minor ailments. A recent study[4] of 9 and 10 year old children found a significantly higher rate of prematurity and immaturity at birth, and of height still below the tenth percentile for age at 10 and 11 years, among intellectually retarded children (with at I.Q. of 70 or less) than among normal children; significantly more intellectually retarded boys had a skeletal age below their chronological age. Other conditions that were more often seen in intellectually retarded children were a major disease or defect, squint and a marked loss of visual acuity, fits since infancy and two or more attacks of bronchitis during the twelve months preceding examination. However, the majority of these conditions were found only in a minority of the intellectually retarded children, and when the children with squint and those with five or more defects were excluded, the differences between the remaining intellectually retarded and normal children were much smaller.

When the 9 and 10 year old educationally subnormal children in the special school were compared with the control group, significant differences were present only in respect of the presence of a major disease or defect, defective vision and stature. The same tendency was seen for a majority of the defects to occur in a minority of the children, and when those with four or more disorders were excluded, there were only slight and statistically non-significant differences in the physical characteristics of the remaining educationally subnormal children and the children in ordinary schools.

Intellectual deficits

A correctly administered test of general intelligence is still the best method of measuring the level of a child's intellectual function. But mental growth is not linear and the I.Q. may not be constant throughout the school years; to this extent an I.Q. at any time may not accurately reflect the life-long potential of a child. Furthermore, to express intelligence in terms of a single quotient is frequently of limited value to a teacher. The strength of a chain is its weakest link and it is more helpful for the teacher to know the strengths and weakness in the child's intellectual functioning than a deceptive expression of overall intelligence that conceals these.

The force of this argument will be appreciated the more it is remembered that a principal requirement of an examination (not least a psychological examination) of a child with difficulty in learning is that it should lead to guidance to the teacher in formulating a constructive teaching programme. Merely to know that a child's I.Q. is below the normal range may mislead the teacher

---

[3] Douglas, J. W. B. (1964). Paper prepared at the request of the Central Advisory Council for Education (England).

[4] Rutter, M., Tizard, J., & Whitmore, K. (Eds.), 1969. Education, health and behaviour. London: Longmans.

85

into supposing that each and every component of the child's intellectual function is equally depressed. Whilst this may be true of some mentally subnormal children it is not true of them all.

The limitations of an I.Q. score are apparent from the use of the Stanford-Binet Intelligence test. This is a very good predictor of whether a child will be capable of academic school learning. Its predictive value is closely related to the fact that the test relies to a great extent on a child's verbal concepts and linguistic skills, which are just those skills that are required for high academic achievement. The test is less satisfactory as an all-round assessment of intellectual potential.

Fluctuations in I.Q. scores over a period of time have often been reported. During 1966–67, two further studies were made in the West Riding. The first[5] reviewed the changes in the I.Q. scores on the Stanford-Binet Intelligence Scale occurring in educationally subnormal children between ascertainment and leaving school. The second[6] included a comparison of I.Q. scores, obtained on both Stanford-Binet and Wechsler Intelligence Scales, of children both under and over the age of 11 years who had been referred for psychological examination because of disturbed behaviour or difficulty in assessment. Both studies found a lower Standford-Binet I.Q. in the older children and this was in part attributed to the increasingly verbal content of the scale with age. (The second study was principally a comparative study of the Stanford-Binet and Wechsler Intelligence Scales and confirmed that the former is the more useful scale to use when examining children under the age of 7 and those who may be severely subnormal.)

In neither of the above investigations was allowance made for the underlying cause of any subnormal intelligence present. In a number of studies carried out by Clarke[7] substantial increases in I.Q. during adolescence and early adult life were noted among educationally subnormal school leavers brought up in adverse circumstances; such increments did not occur in those whose subnormality was due principally to genetic or pathological factors (including brain damage). Clarke[8] has more recently emphasised that such changes among the subcultural group were 'not so much a response to the present as a recovery from the past', being due to the fading of the effect of the early adversity. He concluded that, important though early learning may be, its permanence depends not only on the age of the child at the time of the experience but also on the duration and intensity of the experience. Unless the initial experience is reinfored the tendency is for intellectual deficits arising from early adversity, to some extent, to be made good with the passage of time and subsequent learning. At the same time, other desirable changes in personality have been seen to occur. The fact that such recovery may continue into adolescence supports the current opinion that there are optimal rather than critical periods of learning and indicates that the formative period may extend beyond the early school years. Thus, the situation with regard to the influence of environmental factors (e.g. learning) on the subsequent level of intellectual

[5] Simpson Smith, C. (1965). Changes in I.Qs. of Educationally Subnormal Pupils. Public Health, 80, 4, 201.
[6] Pickles, D. G. (1967). Intelligence Tests and the ascertainment of the educationally subnormal. Public Health, 81, 3, 133.
[7] Clarke, A. M. and Clarke, A. D. B. (1958, 1966). Mental Deficiency: the changing outlook. London: Methuen.
[8] Clarke, A. D. B. (1968). Learning and Human Development. Brit. J. Psychiat. 114, 1061.

function may be closely analogous to that of environmental factors (e.g. nutrition) on subsequent physical growth and stature[9].

This has considerable relevance to the examination of educationally subnormal children whose potential is assessed on the Stanford-Binet Scale. Many of these children come from socially disadvantaged homes providing poor and unstimulating physical and psychological environments for child development. These produce disincentives to school achievement which are continually re-inforced by the restricted pattern of speech and language that characterise such homes. As children move through primary to secondary education academic learning depends increasingly on the use of elaborate forms of speech, vocabulary and verbal concepts, and these in turn aid the process of cognitive development. Restriction in an early phase of development delays or interferes with successive phases, and failure re-inforces failure for these retarded children when penalised in the assessment of their intellectual capacity by the use of a test that leans heavily on verbal content. And yet for these children, perhaps even more than for others, academic learning is far from being all that education has to offer.

These are some of the factors that have to be taken into consideration when making recommendations and decisions about the education of children who have difficulty in learning. They point to the need for caution in the interpretation and use of an I.Q. and the use made of it in advising on educational placement. An early pamphlet[10] issued by the Ministry of Education noted that it was from among 'those whose limited ability corresponds with an intelligence quotient of about 55 to 70 or 75' that children were found for whom the day special school was the most suitable. That was 23 years ago, but the interpretation that children whose I.Q. comes within this range ought to be in special schools lingers on, and it is still not unusual to hear the remark that a child's I.Q. is too high or too low to justify special school placement. Today, psychologists no longer attach over-riding importance to an I.Q. in giving educational advice, and some no longer record the I.Q. in their report. Whilst at present about one-third of children in special schools have an I.Q. of 70 or over, it needs to be stressed that recommendations for special school placement should be made in the light of a child's developmental and educational need at the time of the examination, and not on the basis of an opinion as to educational prognosis by the time adolescence is reached. An I.Q. should be used as a guide to educational need and not as a determinant.

Most of the traditional tests of intelligence do not allow for a differential diagnosis to be made other than between disorders chiefly influencing either verbal or performance skills. In 1961, Kirk and McCarthy[11] introduced the first experimental edition of the Illinois Test for Psycholinguistic Abilities in an attempt to provide a test that would discriminate between some of the separate mental processes that make up the final response of a child to certain items in traditional tests. If this were possible the weak links in the chain of response might be identified and hence lead to more specific prescriptions for remedial education. The I.T.P.A. is based upon a limited scheme of communication: the items in the test have been chosen to test 9 processes postulated in

[9] Tanner, J. M. (1961). Education and Physical Growth. London: University Press.
[10] Pamphlet Number 5: Special Educational Treatment. Ministry of Education 1946. H.M.S.O. (out of print).
[11] Kirk, S. A. and McCarthy, J. J. (1961). The Illinois Test of Psycholinguistic Abilities—an approach to differential diagnosis. Am. J. ment. Defic. 66, 399.

the sequence of events between the receipt of visual or auditory linguistic stimuli and the motor response to such stimuli in the form of gesture or speech. These processes have been termed 'decoding' (the ability to obtain meaning from the stimuli), 'association' (the ability to relate different language symbols meaningfully) and 'encoding' (the ability to express ideas in words and gestures). The result of the test may be represented in a profile of cognitive skills subserving language. The first edition of this test is now available to qualified psychologists in this country, though it has not yet been standardised for English children.

Neurological examination

The I.T.P.A. has been developed for the purposes of identifying psycholinguistic disabilities in children. It does not purport to replace other tests of perceptual-motor function nor is it a procedure for determining the etiology of any such disabilities. It is a function of the neurological examination to elicit history and signs that indicate other areas of disturbed function and allow an attempt at a diagnosis of the condition underlying psycholinguistic disability or any other intellectual, sensory or motor disorder producing difficulty in learning.

In the majority of mentally handicapped children it is not possible to identify a definite cause or disease that accounts for the intellectual retardation. Even in children who are severely subnormal a medical diagnosis is seldom possible in more than one in five cases. Recent developments in the study of the causes of mental retardation have been briefly reviewed by Kirman[12].

For practical purposes in the school health service three principal etiologies of intellectual retardation may be recognised: sub-cultural, genetic and pathological. There may be more than one etiological factor operating in any one child, especially when sub-cultural factors are prominent. Since the discoveries relating to Down's disease and phenylketonuria, there is great interest in the study of chromosome abnormalities and inborn errors of metabolism.

In such cases both genetic and pathological factors are involved and referral to a specialist may be required, not only to confirm the diagnosis and advise treatment but also to provide genetic counselling for the parents.

The importance of searching for evidence of organic disorder is well illustrated by the investigation[13] of 2,275 children in 21 schools for educationally subnormal pupils and one school for the partially-sighted, in Liverpool in 1967. This revealed 2 cases of homocystinuria: both were boys aged 6 and 11 years, and because of the known genetic basis for the disorder their families were also investigated when a third case, a boy of 4 years was discovered.

It is likely that pathological factors have tended to be overshadowed in the past by interest in the general level of intelligence of the child. However, in 100 admissions to a residential special school in Birmingham, Tansley[14] noted strong or moderate evidence of pre-, peri- or post-natal hazard in 65 and a history of physical trauma or severe illness (e.g. meningitis, head injury) before the age of 3 years in 28 children. In a study of 801 children attending 8 special schools for educationally subnormal children in South Wales, Williams and

---

[12] Kirman, B. H. (1968). Mental Retardation: some recent developments in the study of causes and social effects of this problem. London: Pergamon Press.
[13] Burns, R. (1968). Homocystinuria: an investigation in 2,275 children in special schools in Liverpool. Med. Office. 70, 237.
[14] Tansley, A. E. (1966). Studying children 'At Risk'. SS.1.15.

Gruber[15] were able to group the children according to whether they remained in the special school until reaching school leaving age, were transferred back to ordinary schools or were admitted to training centres. From perusal of Forms 2 HP and 3 HP, they were able to study the characteristics of these three groups of children. The details obtained about the children transferred to training centres pointed to these children being appreciably more neurologically handicapped than those returning to ordinary schools, who were more environmentally handicapped. But even among those remaining in the special schools a history of abnormality of the birth process was noted in 24 per cent and a motor defect was found in 9 per cent.

Psychiatric disorders

In determining the factors that contribute to the difficulties some children experience in learning, attention must sooner or later focus upon their social behaviour and an assessment be made of their emotional development and the presence or otherwise of psychiatric disorder.

That children who have difficulty in learning often also have difficulty in behaviour adjustment is well known to their teachers but there has been relatively little study of the relationship. Within the last few years two enquiries have been made. Chazan[16] obtained detailed information about the incidence and nature of maladjustment among 169 educationally subnormal children aged 9–10 and 13–14 years, attending 8 special schools in Wales. On the basis of the Bristol Social Adjustment Guide, over one third had a score of 20 or more (i.e. in the 'maladjustment' range) and the delinquency rate among these educationally subnormal children was twice that among a group of children in ordinary schools. Thirty of the 'maladjusted' children and thirty controls were the subject of intensive investigation: 7 of the 'maladjusted' children had epilepsy, suggesting organic brain disorder might be important in relation to their disturbed behaviour, and disturbed family relationships were more often present than in the control children. These findings were much in line with the results of a retrospective survey[17] of the 10 Newcastle children among those studied in the Thousand Family Survey[18] who attended a special school for educationally subnormal pupils; 9 of these children showed emotional problems (e.g. school phobia, truancy) and one third[19] of them came from homes in which family relationships were disturbed.

The survey[20] of 9–11 year old children on the Isle of Wight also found that emotional and behaviour disorders were commoner among intellectually retarded children and also among those of average intelligence who were specifically retarded in reading, than among the normal child population. This survey provided data about the type of behaviour disorder shown by these two groups and demonstrated that anti-social behaviour tended to be more

[15] Williams, P. & Gruber, E. (1967). Response to Special Schooling. London: Longmans.
[16] Chazan, M. (1964). The incidence and nature of maladjustment among children in schools for the educationally subnormal. Brit. J. Educ. Psychol. 34, 292.
[17] Creake, M. (1965). Problems of subnormal children studies in the Thousand Family Survey. Lancet, ii, 282.
[18] Miller, F. J., Court, S. D. M., Walton, W. S. & Knox, E. G. (1960). Growing up in Newcastle-upon-Tyne. London: Oxford University Press.
[19] Douglas, J. W. B. (1964). Paper prepared at the request of the Central Advisory Council for Education (England).
[20] Rutter, M., Tizard, J., & Whitmore, K. (Eds.), 1969. Education, health and behaviour. London: Longmans.

characteristic of those with reading retardation, whilst in children with a lower than normal I.Q. both anti-social behaviour and neurotic disorders were frequently present. Organic brain disorder was an important factor associated with psychiatric disturbance in the intellectually retarded, but there was also a high rate of disturbance in intellectually retarded children who showed no evidence of organic brain disorder. The mechanism of the association between psychiatric disorder and both intellectual retardation and reading retardation was considered and the findings suggested that anti-social behaviour developed either as a consequence of the educational failure or as a direct result of the same factor leading to educational retardation; it appeared to be very unlikely that reading retardation in a child of average intelligence developed as a consequence of anti-social behaviour disorder. Children with neurotic behaviour alone did not show a higher rate of reading disability than the normal population.

The elucidation of the relationship between poor educational attainment and psychiatric disorder is important but sufficient is already known for school doctors to be alert to the wider problems of backward children. More needs to be done in the way of guidance and counselling for the parents on the management of their backward children. More could perhaps be done for the children themselves. Only four of the Welsh children had attended a child guidance clinic, though the reasons for this were not given.[16] In describing the Newcastle children, Creak[17] expressed some doubt as to the inappropriateness of psychotherapy that is commonly assumed for dull and educationally backward children with behaviour disorders; and Chazan[19] has suggested how such children might be helped within a special school. Several local education authorities now have one school that caters particularly for educationally subnormal children who are also maladjusted.

The Syndrome of Cerebral Dysfunction

The subject of 'brain damage' and 'minimal cerebral dysfunction' in children has been extensively documented but a great deal of misconception still surrounds their educational significance, largely because of the imprecise terminology. Many of the disorders included in the term 'brain damage' are probably not due to injury to the brain; cerebral dysfunction may be a more accurate description of the result of the disorder or deviation but the effect on the child's behaviour and learning are often very far from being minimal.

What seems to be clear is that a certain proportion of children have quite marked difficulty in learning because of impaired brain functioning of a kind that is manifest in one or more of a variety of signs or behaviour which make up a syndrome of cerebral dysfunction.

Some signs may be striking and indicative of a major physical handicap (as in many cases of cerebral palsy); others may be minimal (as in some cases of specific reading retardation). Neurological signs may be conspicuous by their absence. Behaviour deviation may be episodic (as in epilepsy) or prolonged

---

[16] Chazan, M. (1964). The incidence and nature of maladjustment among children in schools for the educationally subnormal. Brit. J. Educ. Psychol. 34, 292.

[17] Creak, M. (1965). Problems of subnormal children studied in the Thousand Family Survey. Lancet, ii, 282.

[19] Chazan, M. (1965). Factors associated with maladjustment in educationally subnormal children. Brit. J. Educ. Psychol. 35, 277.

(as in the hyperkinetic syndrome). Abnormal signs or behaviour may be present alone or in almost any combination; and it is crucial in the examination of children with difficulty in learning that where a major disability is present a search be made for accompanying but less obvious signs of cerebral dysfunction. A single sign, or a cluster of signs and abnormal behaviour, may be due to pathological disease or injury to the brain or to maturational delay; the latter may be transient or lasting. There may or may not be overall intellectual retardation. There are thus no signs that are pathognomonic of the syndrome of cerebral dysfunction, and no one type of 'brain damaged' child.

Rutter[20] has clarified the description of children with this syndrome in a manner which highlights the principal areas of difficulty and the common presenting problems, without departing too far from the concept of a complex of signs and abnormal behaviour, since the overlap in any child may be considerable. Rutter identifies two broad groups of disorder according to whether abnormal functions or a delay in the development of normal function is prominent. The various forms of cerebral palsy and epilepsy are the two main conditions in the first group. The second group includes: specific speech retardation, specific reading retardation, the 'clumsy child' syndrome, the 'hyperkinetic' syndrome, and the 'autistic child' syndrome. In their more specific and more extreme forms the first three conditions may be referred to respectively as developmental dysphasia, developmental dyslexia and developmental dyspraxia.

'The Clumsy Child'

Rebuke is one of the occupational hazards of a school child and whilst this is sometimes warranted there are occasions when a child is unpopular and gets into trouble for reasons outside his own control of which the teacher or parent is unaware. Defective hearing and petit mal are classical examples and to these may be added specific clumsiness.

This is no new syndrome. Over the last 30 years a number of reports on it have been published including one, in 1962, by Walton, Ellis and Court[21] that gave details of five children aged between 6 and 12 years, who had been referred because they were clumsy in their gait and manipulation. Their disabilities had seriously interfered with education in school. Two of the children had previously been diagnosed as mentally retarded, though they were all subsequently found to be of normal or above average intelligence. Three of them had articulation defects but only one of them had serious difficulty in learning to read.

In a survey[22] of 810 8–9 year old children in schools in Cambridgeshire all but one of the children with visuo-motor disability were identified by screening procedures designed to provide normative data on the range of visuo-motor skill in children of this age; 31 children (3·8 per cent) had visuo-motor test scores 2 standard deviations from the mean, though all of them had I.Qs. above 90. Fourteen of the more severely affected children, and 14 controls, were observed for 3 years: only 2 of the handicapped children had made satisfactory progress in school and only 2 of the control children had not. Spelling and

[20] Rutter, M. (1967). Brain-damaged children. New Education, 3, 10.
[21] Walton, J. N., Ellis, E. & Court, S. D. M. (1962). Clumsy children: developmental apraxia and agnosia. Brain, 85, 603.
[22] Brenner, M. W., Gillman, S., Zangwill, O. & Farrell, M. (1967). Visuo-motor disability in school children. Brit. med. J. 4, 259.

arithmetic presented the greatest problem but 2 were retarded in reading. Evidence of peri-natal abnormality was found in 6 children and 2 of these were hyperkinetic.

The writers of the report on the survey commented: 'We can also confirm . . . that when these disorders are present without obvious neurological signs the children affected seldom receive the understanding and sympathy which might be thought their due. . . Such children are often accused of laziness or mis-behaviour, or suspected of being mentally dull. In spite of mounting problems at school, none had been referred to the educational psychologist or the child guidance clinic.'

In fact, one child only had been referred for specialist help, and this was to a child psychiatric clinic because of emotional disturbance rather than difficulty in learning. The inference for teachers and for the school health service is clear. Teachers should refer such children to either the school psychological or school health service as soon as they come to their notice, either as backward or naughty children. School doctors are not qualified to give the more sophisticated psychological tests that help to identify the difficulties of these children but the Stanford-Binet scale combined with a special neurological examination designed for screening procedures should allow the doctor to determine the need for specialist and full psychological examination of a child. Although there is general agreement that some improvement in perceptual-motor skills occurs in many cases in the course of development, it is essential to be aware of the children's difficulties at an early age. A number of reports have now been published describing ways in which teachers may help the children overcome or circumvent their disability. Moreover, when a rational explanation is given of the child's behaviour and his performance at school, parental anxiety may be allayed and the children may less often be unfairly rebuked; in either case, psychiatric disorder in the child becomes less likely.

Specific reading retardation and dyslexia
Two reports were published in 1966 on the subject of progress in learning to read. One of these was Education Pamphlet Number 50: 'Progress in Reading' (H.M.S.O.), in which comparisons were made between reading studies, based on comprehension tests, of children aged 11 and 15 years assessed in five national surveys extending over 16 years. Notwithstanding that the children's reading levels were relatively low in 1948, shortly after the disturbance of the Second World War, the improvement was striking. In 1964, boys and girls aged 11 years reached, on average, the reading levels of children 17 months older in 1948 and the standard reached by half the children in 1948 was reached or exceeded by three-quarters of the children tested in 1964.

The second report[23] described a longitudinal survey, based on the books the children could read, of 714 Kent school children born in 1946. A similar improvement in reading ability was found but 15 per cent were severely backward at the age of 8 and 0·3 per cent were still illiterate at the age of 11 years.

Two cross-sectional studies also provide some measure of the extent of reading backwardness. In a sample of 14–15 year old children of normal intelligence in a secondary modern school in Leeds,[24] 10 per cent had a reading

---

[23] Morris, J. (1966). Standards and progress in reading. London: N.F.E.R.
[24] Lovell, K., Gray, E. & Oliver, D. E. (1964). A further study of some cognitive and other disabilities in backward readers of average non-verbal reasoning scores. Brit. J. Educ. Psychol. 34, 275.

age at least 2 years below their chronological age. In the Isle of Wight educational and medical survey,[4] 7·4 per cent of 2,193 children aged 9 and 10 years had a similar degree of reading backwardness.

Vernon[25] summarised some of the factors associated with reading backwardness which she classified as environmental or individual. The first group included poor teaching or inappropriate methods, overcrowded classes, frequent changes of school or absence, and social factors. The second group included sub-normal intelligence, physical disorders and emotional maladjustment. Dyslexia she discussed under a separate heading.

Frequent illness may interrupt schooling, and poor vision or impaired hearing may make learning difficult. Such physical conditions need to be treated in any child but they were not found to be causally important in the survey of Kent school children. On the other hand, speech disorders were often associated with inferior reading ability through their relationship with language function. Morris did not consider that dyslexia was a separate entity, distinct from reading backwardness due to the many other factors already mentioned.

Critchley[26] re-stated what he called 'the neurological credo' regarding reading retardation: '. . . there exists a hard core of cases, which by definition comprise children who are of normal or even higher intelligence: who are not fundamentally neurotic, inattentive or lazy; who experience in a conspicuous fashion a difficulty in learning the conventional meaning of printed or written verbal symbols and of associating them with their appropriate acoustic properties . . . Great difficulties in writing and spelling naturally follow. This condition is what we call 'specific developmental dyslexia'. It is commoner in males and it is genetically determined . . .' He elaborated this definition in a publication[27] the following year and described how many dyslexic children may have been slow in learning to talk, have spatial defects, disorders of motility (especially inco-ordination) and left-right directional confusion. The evidence for the condition being a genetically determined maturational lag lay principally in the common family history of delay and difficulty in learning to read; similar difficulties that were displayed by brain injured children he regarded as 'symptomatic dyslexia'.

Ingram[28,29] has written extensively on the subject of specific dyslexia and dysgraphia and considers that all children affected have difficulty in relating visual symbols with spoken speech sounds and almost all have in addition either visuo-spatial difficulties or word-sound difficulties.

The two cross-sectional surveys mentioned above throw further light on the problem. In one group of 50 backward readers of normal intelligence selected from 1,205 third-year junior school children in Leeds,[30] a poorer performance on a vocabulary test and tests involving spatial relationships and left-right

---

[4] Rutter, M., Tizard, J., & Whitmore, K. (Eds.), 1969. Education, health and behaviour. London: Longmans.

[25] Vernon, M. D. (1968). Backward readers. London: College of Special Education.

[26] Critchley, M. (1963). The problem of developmental dyslexia. Proceedings of the Royal Society of Medicine, 56, 209.

[27] Critchley, M. (1964). Developmental dyelexia. London: Wm. Heinemann.

[28] Ingram, T. T. S. & Mason, A. W. (1965). Reading and writing difficulties. Brit. med. J. ii, 463.

[29] Ingram, T. T. S. (1965). Specific learning difficulties in childhood. Public Health, 79, 2, 70.

[30] Lovell, K., Shapton, D. & Warren, N. S. (1964). A study of some cognitive and other disabilities in backward readers of average intelligence assessed by a non-verbal test. Brit. J. Educ. Psychol. 34, 58.

discrimination was found than among a control group, and also a larger number of certain types of error in copying words and abstract designs. In a second group of 50 9–10 year old backward readers,[31] an association was found between reading ability and tests of audio-visual integration and motor performance. Both these studies suggested that in some 'ordinary reading failures' neurological dysfunction played some part.

The children in the Isle of Wight survey[4] were described as having specific reading retardation when their reading ability was 28 months or more behind that expected of them in view of their chronological age and individual ability (I.Q. on a W.I.S.C.). Such reading retardation occurred in 86 children (3·9 per cent of the cohort). Ten of this group were reading at a level appropriate for their age and yet more than 2 years behind their ability (i.e. they were reading retarded but not backward in reading). Individual psychological and neurological examination showed that all save one of the features said to be characteristic of dyslexia were also found to be associated with the specific reading retardation of these 86 children. However, there was no clear tendency for such features to be clustered together: many of the children showed some of the features, 49 children showed only one or two each, and only a few showed all of them. Developmental abnormalities were thus confirmed as being etiologically important but the findings did not support the contention of there being one discrete condition of 'specific developmental dyslexia'. Rather they were in line with the view that there may be two or three varieties resulting from varying combinations of developmental neurological abnormalities.

It would seem that the resolution of the contrasting views regarding the existence of specific developmental dyslexia is not a matter of great practical importance, though clearly of interest. If the condition does exist it is still an inadequate diagnosis on which to base a prescription for remedial teaching for not all dyslexics require the same teaching programme. It is also unhelpful if it is so exclusive a diagnosis that normal intelligence is a pre-requisite, for it has been shown[32] that some backward readers among intellectually retarded pupils (Stanford Binet I.Q. 64–68) have similar cognitive disabilities to children with dyslexia. As Vernon[25] has said of all backward readers: 'Even when their particular difficulties are very similar, the causes of these are widely different. These should be carefully investigated, accurately diagnosed and appropriately treated.' And even when a genetically determined, developmental neurological abnormality or maturational lag has been demonstrated, physical, social and psychiatric disorders are commonly present and need to be recognised and dealt with in the total plan of treatment for the child.

The school health and school psychological services face a big problem in the investigation of these children, and the medical role is crucial. Some local education authorities arrange for the examination in these children during the course of the routine work of school doctors and educational psychologists; others, such as Nottingham, provide a special dyslexia clinic. What is certain is that a few national special clinics, such as the Word-Blind Centre, set up by

---

[31] Lovell, K. & Gorton, A. (1968). A study of some differences between backward and normal readers of average intelligence. Brit. J. Educ. Psychol. 38, 240.

[4] Rutter, M., Tizard, J. & Whitmore, K. (Eds.), 1969. Education, health and behaviour. London: Longmans.

[32] Lovell, K., White, C. & Whitley, R. (1965). Studying backward readers. Spe. Educ. 54, 3, 9.

[25] Vernon, M. D. (1968). Backward readers. London: College of Special Education.

the Invalid Children's Aid Association in London, cannot alone meet the need.

'The Autistic child'

The difficulties in learning experienced by autistic children and the problems facing education authorities in providing special education were described in the Health of the School Child for 1962–63, in a chapter on Psychotic Children. Since then a sub-classification of psychotic disorders has been proposed[33] which may prove valuable for those who have to provide for these children. Three main groups are identified according to the age of onset of the disorder: in early adolescence, in the pre-school years and in infancy.

The first variety is thought to be a juvenile form of schizophrenia and distinct from the psychoses arising in the pre-school years. The clinical differentiation of the latter may be exceedingly difficult because some manifestations are common to both types. A history of normal development up to the age of three, four or five years, and the great similarity with the clinical picture of children known to have suffered brain injury, suggests that the pre-school variety in its 'purest' form, is basically a form of chronic brain disease. Hyperkinesis may be a prominent feature.

Infantile psychosis is differentiated by (a) its appearance during infancy and rarely after the age of two years, (b) autism, (c) a profound disorder of language development, and (d) the other features described among the 'nine points' that were considered to be characteristic of the schizophrenic syndrome of childhood, with the exception of over-activity and excessive anxiety. It is unfortunate that 'autism' has been used so freely to refer to both the syndrome of infantile psychosis and one of its prominent features; however, the term 'autistic child' has come to stay if only from common usage.

Local education authorities have been very much more aware in the last 5 years of the problems of ascertainment of autistic children and of their special educational treatment when this has been recommended. The teachers are dependent upon the doctors to provide a precise diagnosis before they can formulate an approach and plan for their education and the lack of knowledge regarding the causation of autism has hampered this process.

Rutter[33] has also reviewed the current concepts of autism and suggested tentatively that the most promising hypothesis to follow is that the autistic child's difficulties arise basically from a disorder of language associated with cognitive and perceptual defects, i.e. cerebral dysfunction. Further support for this view comes from the re-examination after a period of 5 to 15 years of 63 children with infantile psychosis who first attended the Maudsley Hospital Children's Department between 1950 and 1958.[34] The children were on average aged $15\frac{1}{2}$ years when followed up and their social and behavioural outcome were compared with those of 63 children matched for age, sex and I.Q. who attended the Department because of non-psychotic disorders of emotional development and behaviour. Although the generally poor prognosis of this condition was again demonstrated some children had made substantial progress.

[33] Rutter, M. (1968). Concepts of autism: a review of research. J. Child. Psychol. Psychiat. 9, 1.
[34] Rutter, M. & Lockyer, L. (1967). A five to fifteen year follow-up study of infantile psychosis. Brit. J. Psychiat. 113, 1169.

95

One in four had a reading level of 8 years and school attainments were as good as those of the control children although less than half of the psychotic children had more than 2 years of education in school. Prognosis was poor if a child had not gained useful speech by the age of 5 years; on the other hand some children acquired speech after this age and subsequently made appreciable progress, and there was some evidence that this improvement was related to the education they received in school. The I.Q. was found to be important in relation to prognosis, over and above the fact that those with a higher I.Q. had more often been retained within the education system and not dealt with as severely subnormal. Among those children who did not receive education were several with normal intelligence and only mild behaviour disorders. There were fewer facilities for special education 10 years ago than there are now, and no doubt today some of these children would have been in special schools. Mittler[35] and his colleagues have shown that about one third of a group of heavily handicapped psychotic children who received help from qualified teachers employed in a hospital school, were able to return to their ordinary schools and achieve near normal educational attainments. There is, therefore, reason for cautious optimism that education has something to offer these very handicapped children.

Prevalence and placement

In January, 1968, there were 49,175 educationally subnormal children in special schools (40,297 in day schools and 8,878 in residential schools); a further 10,166 children were awaiting admission to a special school (7,589 to a day school), and 238 were receiving special education in their own home, or in other groups, under Section 56 of the Education Act, 1944. The overall prevalence was 8 per 1,000 school children. Comparative figures are given in Table I for 1950 and 1960.

TABLE I

Year	Attending Special School	Awaiting Special School	Total	No. of pupils on Registers of Maintained and Assisted Primary and Secondary Schools (incl. Nursery and Special Schools)	Prevalence per 1,000 pupils
1950	17,351	11,693	29,044	5,698·6	5·1
1960	35,342	11,905	47,247	6,998·9	6·8
1968	49,175	10,166	59,341	7,636·3	7·6

Some autistic and hyperkinetic children are likely to be included in local education authorities' returns of educationally subnormal pupils receiving full-time special education. In so far as some of them may perhaps require a different educational regime and teaching methods from children who are mentally retarded or merely dull and backward, it may be useful to gauge

[35] Mittler, P., Gillies, S. & Jukes, E. (1966). Prognosis in psychotic children: report of a follow-up study. J. Ment. Defic. res., 10, ii, 73.

their prevalence separately. Children with the autistic syndrome were investigated[36] in Middlesex in 1964; their prevalence among 8–10 year old children amounted to 2·3 per 10,000. This was a total population survey and not one that was confined to children provided for within the education system. Even so, the prevalence recorded was likely to have been under-stated, being based upon the number of children firmly diagnosed as autistic. In fact, the enquiry revealed 35 children (4·5 per 10,000) who showed either the features of infantile psychosis described by Kanner[37] or similar disorders of language and perception and social behaviour but with less severe abnormalities of motility, or repetitive, ritualistic behaviour.

Little information is available regarding the prevalence of children with the hyperkinetic syndrome. It is likely that marked over-active behaviour will have been accepted as a behaviour variant of autistic and brain-injured children, ascertained as educationally subnormal. Rutter[20] has stated that this syndrome is to be seen in about one or two per cent of infant school children, and they often have fits also. Ounsted[38] found that as many as 8 per cent of a consecutive, unselected series of children referred to hospital because of convulsive disorders became hyperkinetic. He noted that the syndrome characteristically appeared within a few years of the condition causing the epilepsy, and was usually present by the age of five years. In later school years, hyperkinesis is less evident in these children.

The prevalence of clumsy children and those with specific reading retardation (including dyslexia) can be gauged only from the surveys already referred to, and may, therefore, be in the region of 4–6 per cent. They represent a substantial proportion of the children who are backward for their age in reading. There are no national statistics to act as a guide, the majority of these children do not require full-time education in a special school and therefore now do not appear on local authorities' registers of handicapped pupils as educationally subnormal. Strictly speaking, they are among the educationally subnormal children who require '. . . some specialised form of education . . . partly in substitution for the education normally given in ordinary schools'. Some of these children will be having remedial teaching and others may be attending special classes in ordinary schools, but there is good reason to believe that many receive no special education.

Special educational treatment for handicapped pupils is more a problem for ordinary schools, than special schools, so far as numbers are concerned and for reasons discussed below, it is likely that the size of the problem in respect of educationally subnormal pupils has still not been defined by most local education authorities. The provision of special schools is increasing but there is little sign yet that even this has reached the level required by present-day criteria for admission, since the prevalence of educationally subnormal pupils in special schools, per 1,000 of the school population, continues to rise (Table I).

---

[36] Lotter, B. (1966). Services for a group of autistic children in Middlesex. In *Early Childhood Autism*. Ed. Wing, J. K. Pergamon Press, London.
[37] Kanner, L. (1943). Autistic disturbances of affective contact. Nerv. Child, 2, 217.
[20] Rutter, M. (1967). Brain-damaged children. New Education, 3, 10.
[38] Ounsted, C. (1955). The Hyperkinetic syndrome in epileptic children. Lancet, ii, 303.

The proportions of children receiving full-time special education in 1967 as educationally subnormal pupils per 1,000 children in maintained Infant, Junior and Senior schools, are given in Table II.

TABLE II

Age in Years	Prevalence per 1,000 children in maintained Infant, Junior and Senior schools (1967)
5 6	0·5 per 1,000 Infants
7 8 9 10	5·6 per 1,000 Juniors
11 12 13 14 15	11·4 per 1,000 Seniors under 16 years

There are several explanations for the very low ratio of infants, and the rapidly increasing ratio among children aged 7 to 12 years, who require full-time special education. Teachers are reluctant to label a child educationally subnormal at an age when the attainments of even a normal child have barely reached a level that can be described as an educational performance; they prefer to give a child an extended period of normal schooling at this young age before reaching the conclusion that he is backward; they can be rather more confident about this when the child is aged 7 or 8 years and a reading age can give some measure of backwardness. These attitudes received some support in the past, not only from the views expressed in Pamphlet Number 5 (H.M.S.O., 1946) to the effect that infant school children do not normally require special education unless they are seriously retarded, but also from the fact that local education authorities seldom provide places in their special schools for children under the age of 7 years.

The ratios in Table II might also be interpreted as evidence that ordinary schools do, in fact, cater for educationally subnormal children until an age when their education becomes increasingly academic, as in the secondary school. The highest age specific rates for educational subnormality occur from the age of 12 to 14 years, after the children have had a trial in ordinary secondary schools.

The Isle of Wight Survey data relating to educationally backward children certainly confirm that the urgent quantitative problem is that of providing part-time special education for educationally sub-normal pupils in ordinary schools; 174 children aged 9 and 10 years were educationally backward by two standard deviations or more, but only 38 were in full-time attendance in special units of one kind or another: 27 in a day special school, 2 in a unit for cerebral palsied children and 9 in a training centre or subnormality hospital; the remaining 136 children (6·2 per cent of the age group) were in ordinary schools.

98

On the other hand, the rate of educational subnormality requiring full-time attendance of a child in a special school was 13 per 1,000—almost twice that of the national prevalence among 9 and 10 year old children of 7·2 per 1,000. The Isle of Wight rates were an expression of educational need and not of intellectual retardation: 7 of 29 children in special schools had an I.Q. of 70 or more whilst 28 of 50 educationally backward children with I.Q.s below 70 were in ordinary schools. The 136 backward children in ordinary schools were picked out by a series of screening procedures, and whilst the individual examination of each child by the research team did not suggest that full-time special education was required the children certainly required part-time special education. The schools had been unaware of this, to the extent that, for the majority of the children, such help had not been provided or sought.

Similar evidence of the unexplored need for special education in ordinary schools was produced by the National Child Development Study[39] when a national cohort of children born one day in March, 1958, were re-examined in 1965, in their last term at an infant school. Their teachers were of the opinion that 2 per cent of these 7 year olds would have benefited from attendance at a special school because of their backwardness or difficulties in school; 5 per cent of the group were already receiving some help within the school over and above what the class teacher was 'able to do in the normal way'. However, the teachers thought that a further 8 per cent of the children 'would benefit from (similar) help at the present time. Thus, not less than 13 per cent of this school population were already in difficulties by the age of 7 but two-thirds of them were not receiving any special help and one-third had not even been referred to either the school health or school psychological services for investigation of their problems.

The above figures emphasise again what has often been said of handicapped children in general and of those with difficulty in learning in particular: that identification and assessment need to be undertaken before their difficulties have created serious problems and failure in school.

When there is appropriate special education available, teachers are quick to refer children whom they think would benefit from it; this is clearly demonstrated in areas where special schools for educationally subnormal children admit infant school children, or even children of nursery school age, for the demand never seems to be satisfied. But special school placement should not be the sole objective of referral for special examination; medical and psychological examination may bring to light features about the child that lead to his treatment and constructive advice to the teacher, who gains immeasurably from the better understanding of the nature of the child's difficulties. It could be argued that this is even more important when teachers have to continue to do their best for these children in ordinary schools because a place in a special school is not available.

If the results of specialist investigation were more often communicated to teachers in a form that was of practical assistance to them in teaching the children, the teachers might be more forthcoming with referrals. The school health service has a major share in the responsibility for discovering the children who may need special educational treatment, and when teachers are reluctant to refer the children the school health service must redouble its own efforts.

---

[39] Pringle, K., Butler, N. R. & Davie, R. (1966). 11,000 seven-year-olds. London: Longmans.

The role of the entrant medical examination in this context was stressed in Chapter II. A serious shortage of medical staff hampers ascertainment in many areas, and some local education authorities are still without a school psychological service.

Nursery special classes

It is exceptional for suitable arrangements to be made in ordinary schools for young children with severe learning and behaviour disorders; and many of them require special educational help long before the age of five years. Some of them require a long period of observation and assessment before suitable educational placement can be secured for them. This was recognised in Circular 11/1961, in which the suggestion was made that diagnostic centres might be established to help an authority determine the best form of treatment for each child.

Some authorities have acted upon this suggestion and a number of 'units' have been opened, known variously as diagnostic centres, assessment units or observation classes. A review of some of these units was made in 1966 and 1967 and the results are likely to be published in 1969. It was clear that the exact function of the units had not always been sufficiently anticipated. In some, the main objective was no more than to determine whether a child was suitable for education in school and the prior requirement of comprehensive assessment was overlooked. The difference is important, affecting the number of children that can suitably be accommodated in one group or class, as well as the need for supporting specialist services. In others, the need for these services was fully appreciated but professional staff could not be found.

The significant finding of the survey was the benefit derived by the young children, most of whom were aged 3–6 years, from the activities and help that the teachers were able to provide, although this special educational treatment was seldom the reason why the unit had been established. It is only an exceptionally small local education authority that will have an insufficient number of these children to warrant a special nursery class. The educational value of these classes amply justifies their being set up even when the full range of specialist services are not readily available.

CHAPTER X

HEALTH EDUCATION

Health education in schools is gradually gaining in status and popularity as more teachers perceive its value to pupils. Doctors and nurses from the school health service are increasingly drawn in, sometimes to give talks and sometimes to support teachers. Teachers often feel themselves inadequately equipped to cover the whole field of health education, therefore increasing co-operation between health workers and educationists, who can contribute to one another's knowledge and expertise, is to be welcomed and encouraged. It is significant that interesting developments in health education often spring from the activities of working parties of teachers and doctors and nurses from the school health service. The experience of many local education authorities has shown the value of such a co-operative approach. A recent example is that of Newcastle-upon-Tyne, where a working party produced some guide lines for health education in the city's schools.

Health education officers who, with the exception of two Authorities (Oxford County Borough and Leeds) are employed exclusively by health departments are making an increasingly valuable contribution. Their professional qualifications and experience vary widely and to a large extent determine their role in schools. Some provide a service of visual aids and other educational material. Others give talks and advise on the choice of specialist lecturers. Some are competent to provide in-service training for teachers. Approximately a hundred local authorities now have officers designated health education officers, many of whom have a supporting staff.

School medical officers are showing an increasing interest in health education and some have made notable contributions both in fostering the activities of working parties and in the schools themselves.

A team approach by teachers, supported, advised and supplemented by the skills of school doctor, nurse and health education officer, has proved its value in many schools, though people with additional skills may be of help when education for personal relationships is under consideration.

Health education should be an essential element in a child's general education and is most effective when one member of the staff of a school is the co-ordinator. A variety of studies can throw light on health, and schemes of work can be carefully drawn up and made known to all concerned.

Many schools begin to concern themselves with health education by calling in a visiting lecturer to talk about a subject of topical interest such as personal relationships or drug abuse. However, such a practice may take a subject out of perspective. It also gives the impression that teachers cannot or will not cope with a subject of compelling concern for young people.

On the other hand, a visiting lecturer may bring expert knowledge which is valued by the pupils. Nevertheless such an occasion should be integrated into the normal activities of the school as far as is possible. The visitor might be one of a number of professional people contributing to a leavers' course of a 'Design for Living' or 'Preparation for Family Life' type. A teacher, invited to sit in on a talk, is in a position to integrate the lecturer's material and to carry on in discussion points that pupils raise. If the visitor is the school doctor or nurse he, or she, may well become a regular member of the school health education team, and this is happening in some local authority areas, notably Hampshire. For health workers to undertake the bulk of health education does, however, limit the number of schools which can be served owing to the shortage, and heavy programmes, of school medical officers and nurses: a more economic use of their experience and knowledge might be in the training and supporting of teachers.

There is little doubt that teachers who undertake health education need help of various kinds. In July, 1968, the Department of Education and Science published a revised edition of the Handbook of Health Education.[1] This has been widely welcomed. It contains a comprehensive chapter on drug use written in collaboration with the Department of Health and Social Security.

The Department's annual Easter course on health education continued to be well supported as were those courses provided by the Central Council for Health Education. In 1968 the Central Council for Health Education was replaced by the Health Education Council which also took over the health education activities of the then Ministry of Health. Towards the end of the year exploratory talks were held between the new Health Education Council and the Department of Education and Science.

The Department also had talks with staff of the National Marriage Guidance Council, which undertakes some in-service training of teachers for education in personal relationships. In 1964 it ran three such courses, in 1967, twenty. Attendances by teachers at the National Marriage Guidance Council's Summer School and Work Shop also increased.

The Department's Health Education Panel had useful discussions with the National Marriage Guidance Council particularly about the possibilities of the Council's training teams collaborating with professional people locally.

The Institute of Health Education, the professional body of Health Education Officers, continued to strengthen its links with the teaching profession, to whom its information services should prove extremely valuable.

Continuing education is of great importance to health educators. Wiltshire has its own Association for Teachers of Personal Relationships, which meets regularly for discussions and to hear talks and examine problems.

The London Boroughs Training Committee, established in 1963, has a health education advisory panel for the purpose of making recommendations on appropriate staff training activities in the sphere of health education.

The Training Committee has been particularly concerned with programmes for health visitors, school nurses and health education officers: two pilot projects for medical officers have been organised in association with the Central Council for Health Education. During 1968, 112 staff attended courses which included special reference to health education in schools. These were as follows:

---

[1] Dept. Ed. & Science. A Handbook of Health Education. H.M.S.O. 1968. Price 14s. 6d.

A two-day seminar specifically on this topic for health visitors, school nurses and health education officers; much of the teaching was undertaken by staff from London schools, who welcomed this opportunity. A short introductory course for nurses about to enter the school service included lectures and demonstrations on health education. An advanced course was held for health visitors who were taught principles of group discussion methods which were applicable in a variety of settings, including schools and youth groups. A group of doctors who attended the 'Principles of Health Education' course made a special study of the health education needs of adolescents.

The London Guild of Health Education Officers Ltd. provides a further source of continuing education, but its links with the teaching profession are, as yet, tenuous, though many members work in schools. In 1968 the Guild held a symposium on Trends in Health Education which was attended by teachers, doctors, school nurses and health visitors.

In April, 1967, the Central Council for Health Education with the Society of Medical Officers of Health and The Association of Teachers in Colleges and Departments of Education, held a combined conference to discuss partnership in health education. Delegates made a strong plea for more in-service training, for greater emphasis on health education in colleges of education and for greater inter-professional communication. Following this conference over a hundred lecturers in colleges and departments of education combined to form a Health Education Section of their professional organisation, The Association of Teachers in Colleges and Departments of Education. Representatives of this new Section co-operated with the Department of Education and Science in organising a short course for persons interested in health education in colleges of education, to be held in Oxford, in September, 1969.

The Central Council's Annual Conference in January, 1968, was devoted to the subjects of drug abuse and alcohol. The sociological and pharmacological aspects of the problem were discussed and the conference was very fully supported. Later in the year the Council held a seminar for medical officers of health on Family Life Education. Medical officers found much of the material new and interesting and learned much which would be of value in their own health education activities.

It is encouraging that the inclusion of health education in the training of medical students is under consideration, and that more school medical officers are considering their role in this work and what additional skills they may need to acquire.

Health Education Topics of Particular Importance in Schools

While it is desirable that pupils should have some experience at school across the whole spectrum of health education it is inevitable that certain topics will cause particular concern and receive special attention from time to time.

Cigarette smoking is one of the largest preventable causes of ill health and premature death in the country. It not only causes much avoidable bereavement but is also a cause of considerable financial loss to both industry and the nation.

It is now well established that carcinoma of the bronchus and much chronic respiratory disease and heart disease are associated with cigarette smoking. It is a remarkable social phenomenon that, in view of these facts, education about the dangers of smoking figures so little in many schools and in some not at all.

The Government Social Survey undertook two studies relevant to school-children: one on the smoking habits and attitudes of school boys is to be published in 1969; the other: 'Adults and Adolescents' Smoking Habits and Attitudes' by A. C. McKennall and R. K. Thomas, is already available. These two authors found that the smoking habits and attitudes of parents, school teachers and peer groups influence the smoking habits of the young. This study also found that the minor health effects of smoking such as sore throat and morning cough impressed children. These and other points, which are described in the Department's Handbook on 'Health Education', offer pointers to possible new approaches to the young. There is also much more detailed information in the U.S. Public Health Service report on 'The Health Consequences of Smoking' and in the report of the 1967 World Conference on Smoking and Health, both of which have been sent to medical officers of health of local health authorities.

The Department of Education and Science together with the Department of Health and Social Security are studying the possibilities of producing a tape recording, in association with the Royal College of General Practitioners, which, it is hoped, will discuss the problems of and means of influencing young people. It is hoped also that this teaching aid will be of value to teachers and intending teachers and possibly even to parents' groups.

Drug Abuse

Although in some respects drug abuse may be considered a relatively small problem its rate of increase gives cause for concern. Many authorities have issued leaflets, book lists and other material on the psychotropic drugs. The booklet 'Drug Dependence' by Dr. Anthony J. Wood, published jointly by Bristol Corporation and the Bristol Council of Social Service, is balanced and authoritative. Copies were sent to all local education authorities and many have made use of it. 'About Drugs' by Dr. J. D. Wright, obtainable from the Health Department, 59 Waterloo Road, Wolverhampton, was written for young people. Copies of this have also been sent to all local authorities.

Among the many other authorities which have issued material to schools are Cambridge, The Inner London Education Authority, Portsmouth and Hertfordshire.

In July, 1967, the Department of Education and Science wrote to chief education officers and principal school medical officers concerning the drug problem, asking for any information they had on its extent in their areas. The point was also made that 'The diagnosis of drug use is extremely difficult and there are no specific symptoms and signs whereby it may be recognised with certainty. Whilst it may manifestly affect a child's behaviour in a variety of ways such behaviour may equally be due to causes other than drugs. In so far as the incentive to experiment with drugs is primarily social in origin, though it may ultimately lead to a situation calling for medical, including psychiatric, help, the early detection of drug dependence lies in the early recognition of a measure of maladjustment that warrants investigation.'

The Department of Education and Science has worked in close co-operation with the Department of Health and Social Security and with the Home Office, in considering what may be done about this worrying problem. Children of school age notified as being addicted to heroin, have been very few. Investigation of their cases has, however, shown that signs of serious maladjustment were manifest relatively early in their school life. The main problem among younger people is not with heroin but with the amphetamines and cannabis, as in Sweden.

Observers from the Department of Education and Science attend the Advisory Committee on Drug Dependence and one of the Department's Medical Officers is in close contact with professional workers in the field of drug dependence.

It is not always accepted that children at school should be taught about the dangers of drug use. Clearly the giving of information to school children should not be a crisis measure, but should form part of a balanced pattern of health education.

The Department of Education and Science receives inquiries about the availability of educative material on drug abuse. New material is reviewed and noted as it is published.

Dr. J. D. Wright, Senior Medical Officer, Wolverhampton, conducted a survey of the knowledge and attitudes about drug misuse among fourth year pupils at three Wolverhampton schools. He found[2] that 20 per cent of the respondents knew someone taking drugs; 12 per cent had been offered drugs, and 6 per cent said that they would try them if they were offered. The majority of the respondents said that they had learned about drugs from the press and television. Comparable studies in Sweden suggest a greater problem there of misuse of industrial solvents, cannabis and amphetamines.

Education for Personal Relationships

Education for personal relationships and sex education are becoming an accepted part of education in many schools, and many local authorities run in-service training courses for their teachers.

The Gloucestershire Education Authority pioneered in-service training in education for personal relationships, under the aegis of the Gloucester Association for Family Life. They had the help and advice of persons with relevant professional training, including a psychiatrist and a headmaster. Selection of suitable teachers includes a letter of recommendation from their head teacher and interviews with a psychiatrist and a head teacher. Following selection successful candidates receive a three day residential training.

Wiltshire education authority has held a series of similar courses.

Birmingham ran its first in-service training course for teachers, in 1967, on a different pattern. The course was conducted in co-operation with Birmingham College of Education's one year supplementary course in health education. It offered twelve study days over a period of weeks on sex education, and included instruction in the health services, family planning and drugs. Birmingham have also published an extremely informative pamphlet entitled 'Sex Education'.

Many other Authorities are undertaking similar projects, including West Bromwich, Kent, Cornwall, Lincoln City and Oxford City.

---

[2] Health Education Journal, Vol. XXVII, No. 3.

Local Authorities with General Health Education Schemes of Particular Interest

In Hampshire there is close co-ordination between educationists, doctors and health visitors.

There has been a steady spread of health education with a wide variety of approaches and primary school work in particular is growing. There has also been much contact with parents, who have expressed their appreciation.

In Croydon work is expanding. Courses were given in thirteen secondary and grammar schools. 'Growing up' talks are given to parents and pupils in Junior Schools and half the schools now use this service. Parents are enthusiastic.

In Berkshire, there is a co-operative scheme between health visitors and teachers. Since 1963 the Authority has held conferences on health education jointly with selected health visitors and interested teachers. The principal school medical officer in his annual report for 1964–65 wrote: "The role of the health visitor is that of a skilful group leader—remaining free from dogmatism. She tries to lead and inspire their thoughts and conversation, thus helping them to form and think out for themselves 'right decisions' on the basis of thought for others. The majority of schools ask the health visitor to take one year's course for school leavers, but in some schools health visitors are asked to take classes with eleven year-old and thirteen year-old children as well as school leavers . . 40 health visitors are now working in 30 secondary schools, two grammar schools and two schools for educationally subnormal children."

In Bristol, married women nurses (most of whom have the health visitor's certificate) are employed half-time as school staff nurses, one being attached to each school. They give 80 per cent of their time to individual counselling about health and emotional problems and do much of the health teaching in the schools.

In Northamptonshire, health visitors, supported by health education officers and medical staff, take an active part in health education in schools; one member of the team is a male nurse who is specially concerned with the teaching of boys. Although boys are as much in need of this aspect of health education as girls, it appears that fewer of them receive it in school.

Lancashire has a comprehensive service. The principal school medical officer wrote in his annual report for 1966: 'Health Education should form an integral part of every child's education and any time allocated specifically for this purpose is well spent. It is however not merely a subject which should be presented if there is time; it should be ever present in the minds of teachers, parents, doctors, nurses and all who are concerned with children. The staff of the school health service play a leading part in this work and they are also very conscious of the important part played by teachers, many of whom are doing excellent work'.

Leeds has a team of health education officers recruited from health visitors, who offer a variety of services.

In Oxford City the health education officer's appointment is a dual one, half of his salary being paid by the health authority and half by the education authority. General health education in both primary and secondary schools is well established.

In Ealing, dental health education is being given to infant school pupils.

Sheffield offers a very comprehensive service, financed by the health department. All schools are covered and a health bulletin is sent out to teachers. There is a wide variety of patterns, piloted by a working party on health education in schools. Parent teacher meetings are held and these are often addressed by specially qualified teachers.

In Hammersmith there is a permanent health education exhibition which forms a focal point for health teaching. It covers all aspects of health education and is visited by 500 pupils a week. The Borough also conducts campaigns on special topics.

Many other authorities are active, but space does not permit individual mention of all. The growth and the increasing co-operative nature of health education is much to be welcomed as a valuable preventative health measure. Research and evaluation, however, are still inadequate, and it is to be hoped that the new Health Education Council will make a major contribution to this aspect of the subject.

CHAPTER XI

ACCIDENTS AT SCHOOL

The Department of Education and Science, in collaboration with the chief education officers, principal school medical officers and head teachers, investigated all accidents in the maintained schools of ten counties and county boroughs throughout the three terms of 1965, that caused fractured bones or an absence from school of half a day or longer; accidents not involving absence from school were excluded from the enquiry.

The ten areas had a school population of 833,773 (428,785 boys, 404,988 girls) in nursery, primary, all-age, secondary, comprehensive and special schools; 2,382 were at nursery, and 7,246 at special, schools. The sample comprised just over 11 per cent of the total maintained school population in England and Wales; 489,457 pupils were in urban or predominantly urban, and 344,316 in rural or mixed rural and urban areas.

A total of 4,058 children (2,586 boys, 1,472 girls) were injured at school.

Place of occurrence of accident. Most accidents occurred in playgrounds with playing fields the next commonest site; accidents in gymnasia comprised the third, and in classrooms the fourth, largest groups. There were few accidents in domestic science and handicraft rooms, laboratories, and swimming baths, but more in cloakrooms, corridors, on staircases and steps. Details are given in Table I.

TABLE I

Place of occurrence of accident: rate per 100,000

Place of occurrence	Number of pupils per 100,000 involved in accidents in each of the 10 areas									
	1	2	3	4	5	6	7	8	9	10
Indoor										
Classroom	29·3	35·1	18·3	16·0	29·6	14·6	24·5	35·3	75·2	49·5
Laboratory ..	2·4	—	—	—	7·4	2·6	1·2	5·7	5·4	11·0
Handicraft Room	2·4	14·4	2·8	1·2	—	2·6	5·5	7·9	5·4	22·0
Domestic Science Room	2·4	—	2·8	—	3·7	1·3	1·1	2·8	—	—
Hall (excluding P.E. sessions) ..	4·8	12·4	5·6	3·6	22·3	2·6	9·1	12·3	5·4	11·0
Gym (or hall used for P.E.) ..	119·9	126·1	42·3	33·2	77·0	73·1	53·7	146·6	166·6	77
Corridor	12·2	12·4	7·0	1·2	22·2	7·9	9·1	23·5	10·7	16·5
Staircase	14·6	14·4	4·2	1·2	11·1	5·2	5·1	21·3	16·1	—
Cloakroom ..	19·5	16·5	14·1	6·2	7·4	3·9	6·2	11·7	21·5	5·5
Toilets	—	4·2	7·0	2·4	3·7	2·6	6·2	10·0	5·4	—
Other indoor ..	9·7	8·2	2·8	2·5	3·7	6·6	6·6	11·2	—	11·0
Outdoor										
Playground ..	266·5	272·1	162·1	123·0	200·5	164·8	155·0	249·0	322·4	181·5
Playing Field ..	122·3	157·0	67·6	39·3	115·2	96·2	71·9	79·4	129·0	132·0
Swimming Bath ..	2·4	2·1	—	—	7·4	—	1·5	2·9	—	—
School Garden ..	7·3	6·3	4·2	1·2	11·1	1·3	1·2	6·8	—	—
Other school grounds	12·2	12·4	5·6	3·7	3·7	15·8	9·9	8·4	10·8	5·5
School steps ..	7·3	22·8	7·0	4·9	14·8	2·6	11·6	12·3	—	—
School journey ..	—	2·1	1·4	—	—	1·3	0·8	4·0	5·4	—
Elsewhere	14·7	8·3	7·0	6·1	18·5	15·8	13·5	7·8	10·7	—

Activities the children were engaged in when accident occurred

More children were injured during physical education than other teaching activities; and the accident rates during physical education were considerably higher among the older boys and girls, and higher among boys than girls. Table II gives the details.

TABLE II

Number of Pupils per 100,000 and the activities they were engaged in when accident occurred

Area	Activities	Boys			Girls			Boys and Girls Total
		Under 11	11 and Over	Total	Under 11	11 and Over	Total	
1	2	3	4	5	6	7	8	9
1	P. Ed.	91·8	511·1	271·6	95·2	192·0	115·8	199·5
	Other Teaching	58·4	55·5	57·1	17·4	12·0	15·1	36·6
	Non-teaching hours ..	208·5	344·5	266·8	155·8	252·0	196·1	232·4
2	P. Ed.	91·1	564·3	291·4	105·3	346·9	211·1	252·1
	Other Teaching	14·0	19·3	16·1	7·5	28·9	16·8	16·5
	Non-teaching hours ..	322·6	468·6	384·3	270·8	173·4	228·1	307·9
3	P. Ed.	43·3	239·3	128·3	30·8	121·6	70·0	100·1
	Other Teaching	28·8	18·9	24·5	15·4	6·8	11·7	18·3
	Non-teaching hours ..	130·0	170·1	147·4	133·5	67·6	105·1	126·9
4	P. Ed.	37·5	193·8	103·6	8·6	101·8	47·8	76·2
	Other Teaching	8·4	5·7	7·2	8·6	18·0	7·5	7·5
	Non-teaching hours ..	120·9	68·4	98·7	77·8	18·0	57·7	78·7
5	P. Ed.	48·4	377·2	180·6	50·8	345·8	168·3	174·6
	Other Teaching	36·3	35·9	36·1	38·1	19·2	30·5	33·4
	Non-teaching hours ..	350·7	269·4	318·0	203·2	326·6	252·4	286·1
6	P. Ed.	72·3	362·8	197·6	37·4	193·6	103·0	151·5
	Other Teaching	9·0	—	5·1	9·4	6·5	8·1	6·6
	Non-teaching hours.. ..	225·8	214·1	220·7	107·4	148·4	124·6	174·0
7	P. Ed.	41·1	292·4	144·8	21·6	161·3	78·9	112·7
	Other Teaching	20·5	20·7	20·6	12·7	16·4	14·3	17·5
	Non-teaching hours ..	167·9	184·0	174·5	114·7	97·1	107·5	142·0
8	P. Ed.	120·4	422·6	253·6	86·4	325·3	190·8	223·3
	Other Teaching	25·3	31·9	28·1	12·4	10·6	11·6	20·2
	Non-teaching hours ..	302·9	277·6	291·6	195·2	148·1	174·6	235·1
9	P. Ed.	92·8	580·8	340·8	77·3	128·9	101·0	300·9
	Other Teaching	53·5	24·7	41·5	58·0	26·4	44·7	43·0
	Non-teaching hours ..	267·5	96·9	131·6	193·4	158·4	178·6	188·1
10	P. Ed.	257·4	59·0	257·4	20·2	230·7	494·8	187·2
	Other Teaching	—	23·6	10·7	40·5	—	22·6	16·5
	Non-teaching hours ..	255·7	165·0	214·4	40·4	282·0	147·0	181·7

H   109

Number of children injured and where treated

Of the 4,058 children injured, 363 (9 per cent) had to be admitted to hospital as in-patients; 3,339 (82 per cent) were treated at hospital out-patient departments, or at school clinics, or by their general practitioners; 268 (7 per cent) were treated at school, and 88 (2 per cent) received no treatment. Table III gives the details.

TABLE III

Number of Children Injured and where Treated

Hospital In-patient			Hospital Out-patient department, or by general practitioner, or at school clinic			Treated at school			No Treatment			Total
B	G	Total	B	G	Total	B	G	Total	B	G	Total	
245	118	363	2,125	1,214	3,339	166	102	268	50	38	88	4,058

Length of absence from School

A detailed study of the nature of the children's injuries and the loss of school time they caused was made in the Spring Term of 1965. Of the 4,058 children injured throughout 1965 in the ten areas, 1,770 (1,174 boys, 596 girls) were injured in the Spring Term. Almost half of them were absent from school for only two days or less; only 5 per cent were absent for longer than three weeks. Table IV gives the details.

TABLE IV

Amount of School Time lost in Spring Term, 1965

Number of days	Number of Children
2 or less	813 (46 per cent)
2½–5	491 (27·7 per cent)
5½–10	279 (15·8 per cent)
10½–15	86 (4·9 per cent)
15½–20	37 (2·0 per cent)
over 20	64 (3·6 per cent)
Total	1,770

Nature of Injuries and length of absence from school

Of the 1,770 boys and girls injured in the Spring Term, 1965, 722 (40 per cent) had fractured bones: the percentage was the same for boys and girls. Of the 722 fractures, 386 were of the arms or clavicles, 141 of the legs, 129 of the fingers or toes, and 66 of other bones. No school time was lost by 81 of these 722 children (34 had a fracture of clavicle or arm, eight of leg, 29 of fingers or toes and 10 of other bones); they were either at boarding school or hostel, or had their fracture when attending school on Saturday morning, or returned to school after treatment at hospital because their mother was out working and no one at home till school closed.

110

Cuts and abrasions comprised the second largest group of injuries, involving 567 (32 per cent) children.

Dislocations or severe sprains accounted for 15 per cent of the injuries, being the third largest group (269 children).

Concussion and internal head injuries came next with 98 children (5 per cent).

Eye injuries formed 2 per cent of the total (40 children).

Only 7 had burns or scalds, 6 severe shock, and 5 internal injuries of the trunk.

One child only (a secondary school boy) was injured at boxing. Relatively few boys are now taught boxing at school and their number is declining. Boxing is not compulsory and when taught it is carefully supervised and the boys equally matched; they carry less weight than adults who take part in amateur or professional boxing.

No deaths from school accidents were reported in the areas under review. Details of the injuries received, the numbers of boys and girls affected and the days absent from school are given in Table V.

TABLE V

NATURE OF INJURY AND LENGTH OF ABSENCE FROM SCHOOL IN DAYS: SPRING TERM, 1965

BOYS

Under 11 years

Type of Injury	No. of Pupils	Nil	½–1	1½–2	2½–5	5½–10	10½–15	15½–20	Over 20
Fractures: Arms	94	7	20	19	19	17	4	5	3
Legs	29	2	2	3	3	6	3	1	9
Fingers, Toes	27	4	3	4	8	7	1	—	—
Others	18	3	1	5	2	5	1	1	1
Dislocations, Sprains	37	—	7	5	12	7	1	—	1
Concussion, Internal Head Injury	31	1	1	5	20	4	1	1	—
Cuts, Abrasions	220	—	54	58	68	31	4	—	3
Eye Injury	11	1	2	1	3	4	—	—	1
Internal Injury of Trunk	—	—	—	—	—	—	—	—	—
Burns or Scalds	2	—	—	2	1	—	—	—	—
Severe Shock	3	—	—	2	—	—	1	—	—
Other Injuries	21	1	9	3	4	2	1	1	—
Total	**493**	**18**	**99**	**111**	**140**	**83**	**16**	**9**	**17**

11 years and over

Type of Injury	No. of Pupils	Nil	½–1	1½–2	2½–5	5½–10	10½–15	15½–20	Over 20
Fractures: Arms	157	14	31	25	42	20	14	4	7
Legs	70	2	6	6	16	14	5	4	17
Fingers, Toes	54	13	9	10	9	9	5	1	2
Others	26	4	3	2	10	3	—	2	2
Dislocations, Sprains	122	—	29	30	31	20	6	3	3
Concussion, Internal Head Injury	40	1	4	6	20	6	2	—	—
Cuts, Abrasions	169	—	44	39	56	26	2	1	—
Eye Injury	21	—	6	8	1	1	—	—	1
Internal Injury of Trunk	4	—	—	2	1	—	—	—	—
Burns or Scalds	3	—	1	1	—	—	—	—	—
Severe Shock	1	—	—	—	1	—	—	—	—
Other Injuries	14	—	3	3	4	4	—	—	—
Total	**681**	**34**	**136**	**132**	**194**	**102**	**35**	**15**	**33**

GIRLS

Under 11 years

Type of Injury	No. of Pupils	Nil	½–1	1½–2	2½–5	5½–10	10½–15	15½–20	Over 20
Fractures: Arms	78	5	15	20	16	8	7	1	6
Legs	19	1	1	6	4	5	3	2	2
Fingers, Toes	22	3	5	2	4	4	1	—	—
Others	12	—	1	4	4	4	—	—	—
Dislocations, Sprains	24	—	2	3	3	6	1	1	—
Concussion, Internal Head Injury	18	—	5	3	3	6	—	3	—
Cuts, Abrasions	92	—	24	23	29	12	3	1	1
Eye Injury	4	—	—	1	2	—	1	—	—
Internal Injury of Trunk	1	—	—	—	—	—	—	—	—
Burns or Scalds	—	—	1	1	—	—	—	—	—
Severe Shock	1	—	—	—	—	—	—	—	1
Other Injuries	9	1	2	3	3	—	1	—	—
Total	**280**	**9**	**56**	**63**	**73**	**45**	**16**	**8**	**10**

11 years and over

Type of Injury	No. of Pupils	Nil	½–1	1½–2	2½–5	5½–10	10½–15	15½–20	Over 20
Fractures: Arms	57	8	13	12	16	6	1	—	6
Legs	23	3	1	2	5	2	6	3	2
Fingers, Toes	26	9	4	3	5	4	1	—	—
Others	10	3	1	1	2	—	2	1	—
Dislocations, Sprains	86	2	23	17	23	16	4	3	—
Concussion, Internal Head Injury	9	—	1	2	2	2	—	—	—
Cuts, Abrasions	86	—	20	20	23	17	5	1	1
Eye Injury	4	—	2	1	1	—	—	—	—
Internal Injury of Trunk	—	—	—	—	—	—	—	—	—
Burns or Scalds	2	—	1	1	1	—	—	—	—
Severe Shock	1	—	—	—	—	—	—	—	—
Other Injuries	12	—	5	3	4	1	—	1	—
Total	**316**	**25**	**70**	**60**	**84**	**49**	**19**	**5**	**4**

If the findings of this enquiry in all maintained schools in 10 local education authority areas, containing about 11 per cent of the total maintained school population of England and Wales, in 1965, were representative of all these schools in England and Wales about 35,000 children would have been injured at school that year, involving an absence from school of half a day or longer; about 1,500 would have been absent for three weeks or more; and about 3,000 would have been so severely injured that they required admission to hospital for in-patient treatment.

Supervising active, lively children, especially in playgrounds, playing fields and gymnasia, is onerous at all times, and it is impossible to prevent accidents ever occurring. School doctors should, however, in collaboration with the teachers, study the circumstances under which injuries requiring medical treatment occur in the schools in their area to see if accident prevention measures could be strengthened further.

APPENDIX A

Risk to health from the use of potentially harmful substances in schools

(a) *Lead, arsenic, antimony, barium and cadmium.* In 1965, the Department of Education and Science issued Administrative Memorandum 2/65 that prescribed standards for these substances when used in the manufacture of pencils and allied materials for schools. In 1967, the Toys (Safety) Regulations were made that prescribed standards for these substances in toys.

In 1968, an account was published[1] of lead poisoning in one child, and of raised levels of lead in the blood of several others who had no symptoms of lead poisoning, in a special school for blind children. The affected children were all severely partially-sighted who, unlike blind children who identify objects mainly by touch, also used their tongue and lips to identify objects, including arithmetic type made from metal that was found to contain 65 per cent of lead. They had been using the lead type for a year or longer. This type was to be replaced by an abacus system in the teaching of arithmetic and algebra. The Department of Education and Science immediately drew the attention of the head masters and head mistresses of all schools for the blind and partially-sighted to this report and to Administrative Memorandum 2/65.

(b) *Asbestos.* The inhalation of asbestos dust may lead years later to fibrosis of the lungs (asbestosis), to cancer consequent on fibrosis, or to mesothelioma, a rare malignant tumour of the pleura or peritoneum. Since asbestos was used by children and teachers in some schools (even although not in circumstances likely to create a risk of causing either fibrosis or cancer of the lung in later years) the Department of Education and Science issued, in July, 1967, Administrative Memorandum 20/67 on the precautions to be adopted by schools using asbestos. The memorandum stressed that crocidolite (blue asbestos) should not be used and that the use of all other forms of asbestos should be reduced wherever possible by using a substitute.

(c) *Glass Fibre.* Industrial workers who use glass fibre for the first time sometimes develop irritation and itching of the skin; the irritation soon subsides except in the case of the occasional person who is specially susceptible. In 1967, a report was published[2] of intense irritation and itching of the skin in children and adults from the wearing of clothing that had been machine washed along with curtains made from glass fibre. The machine washing broke some of the glass fibres in the curtains and spread microscopic lengths of the fibres among the other articles of clothing.

Some schools use glass fibres to build canoes. This activity was stopped by one local education authority on account of the alleged risk of dermatitis from handling glass fibre and the resins used to bond the sheets of fibre together. In boat building sheets of glass fibre are covered with adhesive resin and pressed together and into position by rollers. Provided suitable precautions are taken, including removal with an appropriate solvent of any resin that has trickled on to the hands and the thorough washing of hands and arms during and at the end of the work, there is no need to forbid the use of glass fibre and resins in boat building in schools.

---

[1] Ames, A. C., Swift, P. N. Lead Poisoning in Blind Children. Brit. med. J., 1968, Vol. 3, 152–153.

[2] Peachey, R. D. G., Glass-fibre Itch. Brit. med. J., 1967, 2, 221–222.

STATISTICS OF THE SCHOOL HEALTH SERVICE

TABLE I

STAFF OF THE SCHOOL HEALTH SERVICE AS AT 31ST DECEMBER, 1967

| | Medical Officers | | | | | Nurses including Orthopaedic Nurses (see footnote) | Nursing Assistants | Speech Therapists | Physiotherapists | Chiropodists | Orthoptists | Audiometricians | Other School Health Service staff (excluding clerks) |
	Whole time School Health Service	Whole time School Health Service and Local Health Service	General Practitioners working part time in School Health Service‡	Ophthalmic Specialists	Other Consultants and Specialists (other than Psychiatrists)								
Number:													
England	153	1,653	902	256	215	8,233	542	624	270	186	53	128	176
Wales	—	160	46	9	9	590	27	28	3	1	1	5	47
Total	153	1,813	948	265	224	8,823	569	652	273	187	54	133	223
Whole-time equivalent:													
England	135·07	582·44	142·10	55·01	20·44	2,718·01	273·29	413·34	159·69	23·43	18·05	79·93	11·10
Wales	—	61·18	9·83	1·25	0·28	170·80	11·95	21·04	1·95	0·20	1·00	2·17	21·58
Total	135·07	643·62	151·93	56·26	20·72	2,888·81	285·24	434·38	161·64	23·63	19·05	82·10	132·68

Note: The number of Nurses includes 6,215 who hold the Health Visitor's Certificate. (England—5,757; Wales—458)

‡including married women

115

TABLE II

STAFF OF THE SCHOOLS HEALTH SERVICE—CHILD GUIDANCE AND SCHOOL PSYCHOLOGICAL SERVICE AS AT 31ST DECEMBER, 1967

	Psychiatrists	Educational Psychologists		Social Workers		Psycho-Therapists	Other Child Guidance and School Psychological Service staff (excluding clerks)
		Employed in Child Guidance Clinics	Employed in the School Psychological Service	Psychiatric	Other		
Number:							
England	301	422		251	172	89	199
Wales	17	24		5	22	1	40
Total	318	446		256	194	90	239
Whole-time equivalent:							
England	120·68	152·21	203·57	181·60	116·22	54·28	168·75
Wales	9·02	4·50	15·32	4·23	11·06	1·00	26·00
Total	129·70	156·71	218·89	185·83	127·28	55·28	194·75

TABLE III

MEDICAL INSPECTIONS

	Number of pupils on the registers of maintained and assisted primary and secondary schools (including nursery and special schools) in January, 1968	Number of pupils inspected during the year ended 31st December, 1967	
		At periodic inspections	At special and re-inspections
England	7,167,984	1,768,609	1,307,171
Wales	468,306	101,517	57,022
Total	7,636,290	1,870,126	1,364,193

TABLE IV

RECORDED INCIDENCE OF CERTAIN DEFECTS AND DISEASES IN 1967 REQUIRING TREATMENT AND/OR OBSERVATION

Number of periodic inspections in 1967 1,870,126
Number of special inspections in 1967 1,364,193

	Number of defects										
Defect	Periodic Inspections						Special Inspection		Total		Total England and Wales
	Entrants		Intermediate		Leavers						
	England	Wales	England	Wales	England	Wales	England	Wales	England	Wales	
Skin	22,764	1,358	22,994	810	17,931	875	59,897	2,577	123,586	5,620	129,206
Eyes—vision	66,482	3,203	92,717	3,650	70,121	3,308	63,481	3,124	292,801	13,285	306,086
squint	19,750	1,107	10,989	489	3,693	217	6,608	401	41,040	2,214	43,254
other	4,085	251	4,852	156	2,837	188	7,696	152	19,470	747	20,217
Ear—hearing	30,809	1,350	16,346	852	4,877	356	22,348	1,596	74,380	4,154	78,534
Otitis Media	16,824	924	6,985	238	2,837	169	4,144	246	30,790	1,577	32,367
other	5,858	374	3,803	178	2,067	110	7,816	256	19,544	918	20,462
Nose and throat	73,153	4,886	30,554	1,662	9,922	701	21,631	1,594	135,260	8,843	144,103
Speech	23,457	1,243	8,410	455	1,643	136	9,006	717	42,516	2,551	45,067
Lymphatic glands	18,193	1,939	5,837	451	1,188	200	3,267	330	28,485	2,920	31,405
Heart	13,107	1,214	8,096	534	4,255	383	3,817	686	29,275	2,817	32,092
Lungs	24,085	1,473	13,705	679	5,500	398	8,109	801	51,399	3,351	54,750
Development—Hernia	4,721	218	2,116	95	527	40	855	116	8,219	469	8,688
other	18,908	1,177	15,188	523	4,869	284	7,507	572	46,472	2,556	49,028
Orthopaedic—posture	4,606	406	7,037	301	4,746	296	2,188	217	18,577	1,220	19,797
feet	25,509	2,323	18,830	1,022	8,848	584	9,631	592	62,818	4,521	67,339
other	16,338	1,172	11,906	535	7,403	458	8,273	533	43,920	2,698	46,618
Nervous system—epilepsy	2,574	216	2,620	150	1,276	109	1,736	232	8,206	707	8,913
other	6,071	374	4,730	209	1,776	101	4,181	216	16,758	900	17,658
Psychological—Development	10,198	453	13,630	602	3,556	113	12,708	681	40,092	1,849	41,941
stability	23,553	424	18,746	413	4,980	135	14,304	521	61,583	1,493	63,076
Abdomen	6,267	400	5,489	268	2,024	143	2,598	211	16,378	1,022	17,400
Other	17,725	560	21,031	435	9,418	288	60,795	915	108,969	2,198	111,167

TABLE V

NUMBER OF CERTAIN DEFECTS KNOWN TO HAVE RECEIVED TREATMENT BY THE
AUTHORITY OR OTHERWISE, HOWEVER THEY WERE BROUGHT TO LOCAL EDUCATION
AUTHORITIES' NOTICE, I.E. WHETHER BY PERIODIC INSPECTION, SPECIAL INSPECTION
OR OTHERWISE, DURING 1967

	Number of defects treated, or under treatment during the year 1967		
	England	Wales	Total
DISEASES OF THE SKIN: Ringworm—scalp	287	7	294
Ringworm—body	572	23	595
Scabies	10,945	451	11,396
Impetigo	7,862	110	7,972
Other skin diseases	155,005	2,832	157,837
EYE DISEASES: DEFECTIVE VISION AND SQUINT: External and other (excluding errors of refraction and squint)	35,033	645	35,678
Errors of refraction and squint ..	427,179	23,761	450,940
Number of pupils for whom spectacles were prescribed	219,224	11,466	230,690
DEFECTS OF EAR: Number of pupils provided with hearing aids during year	1,736	115	1,851
CONVALESCENT TREATMENT: Number of pupils who received convalescent treatment under School Health Service arrangements ..	7,447	6	7,453
MINOR AILMENTS: Number of pupils with minor ailments	327,948	6,517	334,465

TABLE VI

NUMBER OF CHILDREN KNOWN TO HAVE RECEIVED TREATMENT UNDER CHILD
GUIDANCE ARRANGEMENTS DURING THE YEAR 1967

	Number of clinics	Number of pupils treated
England	348	57,910
Wales	19	3,622
Total	367	61,532

119

TABLE VII

NUMBER OF CHILDREN KNOWN TO HAVE RECEIVED TREATMENT UNDER SPEECH THERAPY ARRANGEMENTS DURING THE YEAR 1967

	Number of clinics	Number of pupils treated
England	1,321	63,473
Wales	99	4,421
Total	1,420	67,894

TABLE VIII

UNCLEANLINESS AND VERMINOUS CONDITIONS FOUND DURING THE YEAR, 1967

	Total number of examinations of pupils in schools by School Nurses or other authorised persons	Total number of individual pupils found to be infested	Number of individual pupils in respect of whom were issued:	
			Cleaning Notices under Section 54(2) of the Education Act, 1944	Cleansing Orders under Section 54(3) of the Education Act, 1944
England ..	10,369,395	182,798	32,872	8,232
Wales	742,463	11,278	2,303	35
Total	11,111,858	194,076	35,175	8,267

TABLE IX

DEATHS BY CAUSE AT AGES UNDER 15 DURING THE YEAR ENDED 31ST DECEMBER, 1967

ENGLAND AND WALES

Causes of death:	Under 5 years of age		5–14 years of age		Total		Total Male and Female
	M	F	M	F	M	F	
ALL CAUSES ..	10,100	7,740	1,559	973	11,659	8,713	20,372
1. Tuberculosis, respiratory ..	6	1	—	—	6	1	7
2. Tuberculosis, other	9	9	—	2	9	11	20
2. Syphilitic disease ..	—	1	1	1	1	2	3
4. Diphtheria.. ..	—	—	—	—	—	—	—
5. Whooping Cough	16	11	—	—	16	11	27
6. Meningococcal infections ..	31	25	4	1	35	26	61
7. Acute poliomyelitis	—	—	—	—	—	—	—
8. Measles	42	31	13	5	55	36	91
9. Other infective and parasitic diseases	61	63	19	23	80	86	166
Malignant neoplasm:							
10. Stomach	—	—	1	—	1	—	1
11. Lungs, Bronchus	2	—	—	2	2	2	4
12. Breast	—	—	—	—	—	—	—
13. Uterus	—	2	—	—	—	2	2
14. Other malignant and lymphatic neo-plasms	120	98	134	118	254	216	470
15. Leukaemia, aleukaemia ..	81	58	108	79	189	137	326
16. Diabetes	3	3	9	8	12	11	23
17. Vascular lesions of nervous system	24	12	13	17	37	29	66
18. Coronary disease, angina	1	—	—	1	1	1	2
19. Hypertension with heart disease ..	—	—	—	—	—	—	—
20. Other heart disease	31	25	18	12	49	37	86
21. Other circulatory disease	10	5	3	1	13	6	19
22. Influenza	6	4	2	3	8	7	15
23. Pneumonia ..	1,472	1,154	82	68	1,554	1,222	2,776
24. Bronchitis	270	207	17	15	287	222	509
25. Other diseases of the respiratory system	135	93	12	11	147	104	251
26. Ulcer of stomach or duodenum ..	2	4	2	2	4	6	10
27. Gastritis, enteritis or diarrhoea ..	269	213	6	11	275	224	499
28. Nephritis and nephrosis ..	11	9	17	16	28	25	53
29. Hyperplasia of pros-tate	—	—	—	—	—	—	—
30. Pregnancy, child-birth, abortion	—	—	—	—	—	—	—
31. Congenital mal-formations ..	1,842	1,623	103	102	1,945	1,725	3,670
32. Other defined and ill-defined diseases	4,898	3,579	279	171	5,177	3,750	8,927
33. Motor vehicle accidents ..	192	97	325	143	517	240	757
34. All other accidents	529	379	379	150	908	529	1,437
35. Suicide	—	—	3	—	3	—	3
36. Homicide, opera-tions of war ..	37	34	9	11	45	45	91

TABLE X

	Net expenditure to be met from grants and rates (excluding loan charges and capital expenditure from revenue) (£000)
England	19,565
Wales	1,293
Total	20,858

TABLE XI

Numbers of corrected notifications of infectious diseases among children under 15 during the year ended 31st December, 1967

England and Wales

| | Scarlet Fever | | Whooping Cough | | Acute Poliomyelitis | | | | Measles | | Diphtheria | | Acute Pneumonia | | Dysentery | |
| | | | | | Paralytic | | Non-paralytic | | | | | | | | | |
	M	F	M	F	M	F	M	F	M	F	M	F	M	F	M	F
Under 5 years	3,294	3,028	9,667	10,377	5	4	—	1	141,931	136,357	3	—	613	453	3,980	3,449
5–14 years	5,790	6,183	5,764	6,768	—	1	1	1	89,334	85,601	1	—	407	324	3,968	3,539
Total ..	9,084	9,211	15,431	17,145	5	5	1	2	231,265	221,958	4	—	1,020	777	7,948	6,988

| | Smallpox | | Acute Encephalitis | | | | Enteric or typhoid fever | | Paratyphoid fever | | Tuberculosis | | Meningococcal infection | | Food poisoning | |
| | | | Infective | | Post-infective | | | | | | | | | | | |
	M	F	M	F	M	F	M	F	M	F	M	F	M	F	M	F
Under 5 years	—	1	10	7	18	13	9	6	6	5	286	279	101	67	576	501
5–14 years ..	—	—	19	13	34	22	29	5	7	10	429	408	37	24	514	484
Total ..	—	1	29	20	52	35	38	11	13	15	715	687	138	91	1,090	985

TABLE XII

School Milk and Meals

Number of day pupils taking dinners in maintained and assisted primary and secondary schools (including nursery and special schools) with percentages based on the number of pupils present on the day of the return; also the number of pupils taking milk

School dinners—1967

			Number of pupils taking dinners			Dinners on payment per cent of number present	Free dinners per cent of number present	Total dinners cent of number present
			Payment	Free	Total			
England	..	..	4,202,160	368,610	4,570,770	64·2	5·6	69·8
Wales	..	..	240,311	35,426	275,737	55·9	8·2	64·1
Total	..	..	4,442,471	404,036	4,846,507	63·7	5·8	69·5

School Milk—1967

			Number of pupils taking milk
England	..		5,626,425
Wales	..	..	343,246
Total	..	..	5,969,671

APPENDIX C

STATISTICS OF THE SCHOOL DENTAL SERVICE

TABLE I

STAFF OF THE SCHOOL DENTAL SERVICE AS AT 31ST DECEMBER, 1967

	Dental Officers (Excl. M. & C.W.)	Dental Auxiliaries (Excl. M. & C.W.)	Dental Surgery Assistants	Dental Hygienists (Excl. M. & C.W.)	Dental Technicians	Dental Health Education Officers	Other staff
Number:							
England	1,707	153	1,682	17	109	25	132
Wales	114	9	101	1	3	1	10
Total	1,821	162	1,783	18	112	26	142
Whole-time equivalent:							
England	1,195·64	133·37	1,470·97	14·44	94·00	10·15	98·02
Wales	76·57	7·48	69·62	—	2·95	1·00	8·90
Total	1,272·21	140·85	1,540·59	14·44	96·95	11·15	106·92

TABLE II

INSPECTION AND TREATMENT DURING THE YEAR ENDED 31ST DECEMBER, 1967

(A) NUMBER OF PUPILS

Number of pupils on registers in January, 1968=7,636,290

	First inspection			Number found to require treatment	Number offered treatment	Number actually treated	% age of pupils found to require treatment who received it	Number of pupils re-inspected at School or Clinic	Number of re-inspected pupils found to require treatment	Attendances made by pupils for treatment
	At school	At clinic	Total							
England	3,486,303	576,004	4,062,307	2,278,047	1,992,461	1,207,744	53·02	415,886	247,125	3,171,058
Wales	165,453	42,857	208,310	138,659	125,809	79,712	57·48	18,479	12,123	190,170
Total	3,651,756	618,861	4,270,617	2,416,706	2,118,270	1,287,456	53·27	434,365	259,248	3,361,228

TABLE II—*continued*

(B) DENTAL TREATMENT (OTHER THAN ORTHODONTIC TREATMENT)—SEE TABLE II(C)—DURING THE YEAR ENDED 31ST DECEMBER, 1967

	Sessions devoted to			Number of fillings		Number of teeth filled		Number of extractions		Teeth otherwise conserved
	Treatment	Inspection	Dental Health Hygiene	Permanent teeth	Deciduous teeth	Permanent teeth	Deciduous teeth	Permanent teeth	Deciduous teeth	
England	501,256	35,087	15,615	1,888,547	744,033	1,598,712	655,190	259,306	810,105	184,173
Wales	33,056	1,928	1,363	119,001	32,924	97,158	29,362	22,377	62,220	12,955
Total	534,312	37,015	16,978	2,007,548	776,957	1,695,870	684,552	281,683	872,325	197,128

	Crowns	Inlays	Teeth root filled	Dentures		Number of pupils X-rayed	Prophylaxis	Number of general anaesthetics administered by	
				Number of pupils supplied with dentures	Number of dentures supplied			Dental Officers	Medical Practitioners
England	4,791	975	5,980	6,120	7,370	71,628	300,165	108,598	245,092
Wales	183	38	655	545	615	2,949	16,533	5,464	27,864
Total	4,974	1,013	6,635	6,665	7,985	74,577	316,698	114,062	272,956

TABLE II—*continued*

(c) ORTHODONTIC TREATMENT DURING THE YEAR ENDED 31ST DECEMBER, 1967

	Number of cases				Number of appliances fitted		Number of pupils referred to Hospital Consultants
	Commenced during the year	Brought forward from the previous year	Completed during the year	Discontinued during the year	Removable	Fixed	
England	23,754	39,602	16,290	3,737	35,661	1,909	4,510
Wales	1,268	2,463	948	241	1,444	271	250
Total	25,022	42,065	17,238	3,978	37,105	2,180	4,760

TABLE III

ATTENDANCES AND TREATMENT BY AGE GROUPS DURING THE YEAR ENDED 31ST DECEMBER, 1967

	Ages 5–9		Ages 10–14		Ages 15 and over		Total		Total England and Wales
	England	Wales	England	Wales	England	Wales	England	Wales	
Number of first visits (i.e. pupils treated) ..	613,359	42,099	499,502	30,846	94,883	6,767	1,207,744	79,712	1,287,456
Subsequent visits	780,494	44,622	974,988	52,161	207,832	13,675	1,963,314	110,458	2,073,772
Total visits	1,393,853	86,721	1,474,490	83,007	302,715	20,442	3,171,058	190,170	3,361,228
Additional courses of treatment commenced	72,245	3,002	61,202	2,493	11,825	562	145,272	6,057	151,329
Fillings in permanent teeth	491,352	30,566	1,113,013	68,141	284,182	20,294	1,888,547	119,001	2,007,548
Fillings in deciduous teeth	682,225	30,038	61,808	2,886	—	—	744,033	32,924	776,957
Permanent teeth filled	399,334	23,665	952,411	56,455	246,967	17,038	1,598,712	97,158	1,695,870
Deciduous teeth filled	601,251	26,966	53,939	2,396	—	—	655,190	29,362	684,552
Permanent teeth extracted	40,605	3,596	179,920	14,498	38,781	4,283	259,306	22,377	281,683
Deciduous teeth extracted	633,906	49,533	176,199	12,687	—	—	810,105	62,220	872,325
General anaesthetics	230,535	22,546	111,677	9,460	11,478	1,322	353,690	33,328	387,018
Emergencies (treatment)	86,083	4,802	44,492	2,423	8,132	633	138,707	7,858	146,565
Courses of treatment completed ..	—	—	—	—	—	—	1,047,972	56,886	1,104,858

129

TABLE IV

Prosthetics 1967 (by age groups)

		Ages 5–9	Ages 10–14	Ages 15 and over	Total
Pupils supplied with Full Upper or Full Lower Dentures for the first time	England	35	89	128	252
	Wales	3	14	20	37
	Total ..	38	103	148	289
Pupils supplied with other Dentures for the first time	England	427	3,525	1,916	5,868
	Wales	30	256	222	508
	Total ..	457	3,781	2,138	6,376
Number of dentures supplied	England	498	4,287	2,585	7,370
	Wales	34	292	289	615
	Total ..	532	4,579	2,874	7,985

APPENDIX D

HANDICAPPED PUPILS REQUIRING AND RECEIVING EDUCATION IN SPECIAL SCHOOLS APPROVED UNDER SECTION 9(5) OF THE EDUCATION ACT, 1944: RECEIVING EDUCATION IN INDEPENDENT SCHOOLS, IN SPECIAL CLASSES AND UNITS; BOARDED IN HOMES AND RECEIVING EDUCATION IN ACCORDANCE WITH SECTION 56 OF THE EDUCATION ACT

ENGLAND AND WALES

	Blind	Partially Sighted	Deaf	Partially Hearing	Physically Handicapped	Delicate	Maladjusted	E.S.N.	Epileptic	Suffering from Speech defects	Total
1. During the year ending 31st December, 1967, number of handicapped pupils who were:											
A. Newly assessed as needing special educational treatment at special schools or in boarding homes	126	341	382	504	1,817	3,195	2,851	11,916	223	62	21,417
B. Newly placed in special schools (other than hospital special schools) or boarding homes	108	324	348	490	1,704	2,847	2,461	10,625	182	46	19,135
2. In January, 1968, number of handicapped children who were:											
A. Requiring places in special schools (i) Day	1	71	46	97	400	285	116	7,589	6	1	8,612
(ii) Boarding	117	120	102	106	321	586	1,203	2,577	49	60	5,241
B. On the registers of maintained special schools (i) Day	17	1,044	1,132	896	5,536	5,034	1,611	40,074	162	54	55,560
(ii) Boarding	178	413	391	422	1,066	2,094	1,770	7,557	119	2	14,012
C. On the registers of non-maintained special schools (i) Day	21	19	155	56	201	—	10	223	—	—	685
(ii) Boarding	945	457	1,298	491	1,308	769	924	1,321	461	81	8,055
D. On the registers of independent schools under arrangements made by local education authorities	5	6	187	113	361	146	2,592	623	5	6	4,044
E. Boarded in Homes and not already included in 2B, C or D above	2	1	5	—	18	144	714	5	—	—	889
F. Being educated under arrangements made in accordance with Section 56 of the Education Act, 1944 (i) in hospitals	—	—	—	—	932	374	197	31	5	—	1,539
(ii) in other groups	—	3	9	16	241	87	317	16	—	3	692
(iii) at home	11	10	8	19	1,046	309	271	191	35	8	1,908
G. Being educated in special classes or units not forming part of special schools	—	104	—	1,709	326	141	1,692	—	—	—	3,972
Total receiving special educational treatment and awaiting places	1,297	2,248	3,333	3,925	11,756	9,969	11,417	60,207	842	215	105,209

(a) During 1967, 2,624 children were reported to Local Health Authorities as unsuitable for education under Section 57(4) of the Education Act.

(b) In January, 1968, 3,873 pupils were on the registers of hospital special schools but not included in the above table.

APPENDIX E

MEDICAL AND DENTAL STAFFS OF THE DEPARTMENT OF EDUCATION AND SCIENCE

Medical Officers

*Chief Medical Officer**
Sir George Godber, K.C.B., D.M., F.R.C.P., D.P.H.

Senior Principal Medical Officer
P. Henderson, C.B., M.D., D.P.H.

Senior Medical Officers
Miss E. E. Simpson, M.D., B.S., M.R.C.P., D.P.H., D.C.H.
T. K. Whitmore, M.R.C.S., L.R.C.P., D.C.H.

Medical Officers
J. N. Horne, M.A., M.D., M.R.C.P., M.R.C.S., D.C.H.
Miss M. Scott Stevenson, M.B., Ch.B., D.P.H.
Miss S. R. Fine, M.B., Ch.B., D.P.H., D.C.H., Barrister-at-Law
Miss E. Wales, M.B., B.S., D.P.H., D.C.H., D.Obst.R.C.O.G.
Mrs. J. D. Dawkins, M.A., B.M., B.Ch.
Mrs. M. W. Jenkins, B.Sc., M.B., B.Ch., D.P.H.†
Mrs. E. Britain, M.B., B.S., D.P.H.

Dental Officers

*Chief Dental Officer **
Surgeon Rear-Admiral (D.) W. Holgate, C.B., O.B.E., L.D.S., F.D.S., R.C.S.

*Senior Dental Officer**
J. Rodgers, D.F.M., L.D.S., R.F.P.S.

Dental Officers
A. T. Wynne, M.B., Ch.B., B.D.S., F.D.S., R.C.S.
J. G. Potter, L.D.S., R.F.P.S.
W. G. Everett, L.D.S., R.C.S.

*These officers are jointly employed by the Department of Health and Social Security and the Department of Education and Science

†This officer is jointly employed by the Welsh Board of Health and the Department of Education and Science

SCHOOL HEALTH AND DENTAL SERVICES

TABLE SHOWING THE NAMES OF THE PRINCIPAL SCHOOL MEDICAL OFFICERS AND THE PRINCIPAL SCHOOL DENTAL OFFICERS EMPLOYED BY EACH LOCAL EDUCATION AUTHORITY, TOGETHER WITH THE NUMBER OF PUPILS ON THE REGISTERS OF MAINTAINED AND ASSISTED PRIMARY AND SECONDARY SCHOOLS (INCLUDING NURSERY AND SPECIAL SCHOOLS) IN JANUARY, 1968.

ENGLAND (COUNTIES)

Local Education Authority	Name of Principal School Medical Officer	Name of Principal School Dental Officer	No. of Pupils on Registers January, 1968
Bedfordshire	M. C. Macleod	H. W. S. Sheasby	45,318
Berkshire ..	D. E. Cullington	O. Jacob	77,890
Buckinghamshire	J. J. A. Reid ..	C. H. Griffiths	92,132
Cambridgeshire and Isle of Ely ..	M. E. Hocken		43,036

132

Local Education Authority	Name of Principal School Medical Officer	Name of Principal School Dental Officer	No. of Pupils on Registers January, 1968
Cheshire	B. G. Gretton-Watson	T. B. Dowell	167,170
Cornwall	H. Binysh	C. A. Reynolds	51,309
Cumberland	J. Leiper	R. B. Neal	39,009
Derbyshire	J. B. S. Morgan	H. E. Gray	119,251
Devon	J. Lyons	F. H. Stewart	68,796
Dorset	A. F. Turner	J. S. MacLachlan	49,871
Durham	S. Ludkin	Mrs. M. M. Lishman	164,042
Essex	J. A. C. Franklin	J. C. Timmis	183,262
Gloucestershire	A. Withnell	J. F. A. Smyth	86,523
Hampshire	I. A. MacDougall	C. C. Chadwick	147,698
Herefordshire	J. S. Cookson	O. S. Bennett	22,269
Hertfordshire	G. W. Knight	A. H. Millett	154,759
Huntingdon and Peterborough	G. Nisbet	I. O. Pinkham	32,293
Isle of Wight	R. K. Machell	G. Simons	13,989
Isles of Scilly	W. D. Bell	B. I. Fairest	259
Kent	A. Elliott	E. Millward	201,206
Lancashire	S. C. Gawne	L. B. Corner	382,972
Leicestershire	A. R. Buchan	D. M. Hobbs	72,195
Lincs.—Holland	J. Fielding	K. Jackson	16,674
„ —Kesteven	E. W. G. Birch	J. E. Mann	24,030
„ —Lindsey	C. D. Cormac	J. Watson	62,168
Norfolk	A. G. Scott	N. J. Rowland	60,384
Northamptonshire	W. J. McQuillan	P. W. Gibson	50,431
Northumberland	J. B. Tilley	A. E. Robinson	81,043
Nottinghamshire	H. I. Lockett	K. H. Davis	107,393
Oxfordshire	M. J. Pleydell	T. Lucas	38,823
Rutland	R. A. Matthews	Miss J. G. Campbell	4,259
Shropshire	P. C. Moore	C. D. Clarke	52,440
Somerset	A. Parry Jones	Q. A. Davies	82,275
Staffordshire	G. Ramage	W. McKay	115,532
Suffolk East	S. T. G. Gray	C. D. MacPherson	33,635
„ West	D. A. McCracken	S. H. Pollard	21,902
Surrey	J. Drummond	O. H. Minton	135,941
Sussex, East	J. A. G. Watson	C. K. F. Evans	50,525
„ West	T. McL. Galloway	P. S. R. Conron	67,243
Warwickshire	G. H. Taylor	H. J. Bastow	95,793
Westmorland	J. A. Guy	M. D. McGarry	10,235
Wiltshire	C. D. L. Lycett	D. Middleton	79,770
Worcestershire	J. W. Pickup	C. W. D. Jones	64,000
Yorks, East Riding	W. Ferguson	G. R. Smith	36,841
„ North Riding	J. T. A. George	Miss A. Potts	69,229
„ West Riding	R. W. Elliott	H. Taylor	290,333

ENGLAND (COUNTY BOROUGHS)

Barnsley	G. A. W. Neill	G. White	14,386
Barrow-in-Furness	A. W. Hay	D. J. Harrison	10,968
Bath	R. M. Ross	G. G. Davis	11,996
Birkenhead	P. O. Nicholas	W. M. Shaw	23,723
Birmingham	E. L. M. Millar	F. J. Hastilow	188,680
Blackburn	J. Ardley	J. Rigby	17,051
Blackpool	D. W. Wauchob	M. Smith	18,890
Bolton	A. I. Ross	A. E. Shaw	25,393
Bootle	G. T. MacCulloch	D. N. Maxfield	16,005
Bournemouth	W. Fielding	Mrs. M. B. Redfern	17,266

Local Education Authority	Name of Principal School Medical Officer	Name of Principal School Dental Officer	No. of Pupils on Registers January, 1968
Bradford	W. Turner	M. J. M. Mackay ..	52,463
Brighton	W. S. Parker ..	W. H. Garland ..	21,120
Bristol	R. C. Wofinden ..	J. McCaig ..	67,149
Burnley	L. J. Collins ..	C. F. Tehan ..	13,996
Burton-upon-Trent ..	R. Mitchell ..	A. N. Stannard ..	10,294
Bury	G. A. Levell ..	F. J. Heap ..	9,879
Canterbury	M. Smith Harvey ..	B. J. West ..	6,927
Carlisle	J. L. Rennie ..	H. W. Freer ..	11,985
Chester	D. F. Morgan ..	G. H. Stout ..	10,540
Coventry	T. M. Clayton ..	J. A. Smith ..	57,625
Darlington	J. V. Walker ..	P. Waterfall ..	13,901
Derby	V. N. Leyshon ..	F. Grossman ..	20,503
Dewsbury	T. W. Robson ..	J. R. Tuxford..	9,907
Doncaster	D. R. Martin ..	A. D. Anderson ..	15,854
Dudley	G. M. Reynolds ..	Mrs. J. P. McEwan	28,147
Eastbourne	K. O. A. Vickery ..	M. G. Berry ..	7,107
Exeter	E. D. Irvine ..	A. Pryor ..	12,841
Gateshead	D. F. Henley ..	Miss T. M. Rossi ..	15,968
Gloucester.. ..	P. T. Regester ..	J. P. Wilson ..	17,123
Great Yarmouth ..	R. G. Newberry ..	B. C. Clay ..	8,880
Grimsby	R. Glenn ..	G. S. Watson ..	18,025
Halifax	J. G. Cairns ..	W. E. Crosland ..	15,664
Hartlepool	H. C. Milligan ..	Mrs. K. M. Atkinson	18,801
Hastings	T. H. Parkman ..	Mrs. Elizabeth M. Ward	8,726
Huddersfield	J. S. W. Brierley ..	J. A. E. Morris ..	21,309
Ipswich	B. A. Smith ..	G. A. Scivier ..	19,372
Kingston-upon-Hull ..	A. Hutchison ..	J. C. Carr ..	54,329
Leeds	D. B. Bradshaw ..	J. Miller ..	82,604
Leicester	B. J. L. Moss ..	E. T. Cunnell ..	49,999
Lincoln	R. D. Haigh ..	G. A. Vega ..	13,215
Liverpool	A. B. Semple ..	P. E. Goward ..	123,502
Luton	R. M. Dykes ..	J. W. Coombs ..	27,093
Manchester	K. Campbell ..	G. L. Lindley..	104,368
Newcastle-upon-Tyne ..	R. Pearson ..	J. C. Brown ..	38,337
Northampton	W. Edgar ..	P. W. J. L. Thompson	19,662
Norwich	J. R. Murdock ..	P. I. Christensen ..	18,813
Nottingham	F. E. James ..	N. H. Whitehouse ..	53,353
Oldham	B. Gilbert ..	J. Fenton ..	18,229
Oxford	J. F. Warin ..	C. H. I. Millar ..	15,777
Plymouth	T. A. I. Rees ..	T. S. Longworth ..	38,648
Portsmouth	P. G. Roads ..	P. D. Bristow.. ..	29,188
Preston	C. F. W. Fairfax ..	A. Kershaw ..	17,679
Reading	A. Gatherer ..	D. O. Mallam ..	21,158
Rochdale	R. G. Murray ..	H. W. Pritchard ..	14,637
Rotherham	I. F. Ralph ..	Miss J. H. Egan ..	15,548
St. Helens	J. H. E. Baines ..	J. P. H. Donovan ..	18,325
Salford	D. J. Roberts ..	E. Rose ..	25,487
Sheffield	C. H. Shaw ..	E. Copestake ..	84,102
Solihull	I. M. McLachlan ..	E. F. Stonehouse ..	17,360
Southampton	A. McGregor ..	A. J. Edwards ..	36,214
Southend-on-Sea ..	G. V. Griffin ..	E. C. Austen ..	24,628
Southport	G. N. M. Wishart ..	W. L. Rothwell ..	11,465
South Shields	I. D. Leitch ..	T. W. Clarkson ..	19,060
Stockport	A. R. M. Moir ..	Miss F. Sellers ..	22,819
Stoke-on-Trent	J. S. Hamilton ..	G. T. Emery ..	46,505
Sunderland	J. MacLachlan ..	F. J. Lishman ..	39,816
Teesside	R. J. Donaldson ..	R. C. Blackmore ..	
Torbay	D. K. McTaggart ..	G. J. Derbyshire ..	

Local Education Authority	Name of Principal School Medical Officer	Name of Principal School Dental Officer	No. of Pupils on Registers January, 1968
Tynemouth	G. MacA. Dowson ..	N. A. Eddy	13,072
Wakefield	G. Firth	R. E. Whittam ..	9,267
Wallasey	H. W. Hall	W. J. Meakin.. ..	16,545
Walsall	J. C. Talbot	Mrs. I. M. Millar ..	31,585
Warley	R. J. Dodds	J. Charlton	24,941
Warrington	E. H. Moore	A. P. Finlay	12,772
West Bromwich	H. O. M. Bryant ..	J. B. C. Cuzner ..	29,479
Wigan	J. H. Hilditch ..	S. M. Aalen	12,876
Wolverhampton	F. N. Garratt.. ..	S. Awath-Behari ..	47,189
Worcester	G. M. O'Donnell ..	E. R. Dowland ..	12,195
York	S. R. W. Moore ..	G. Turner	17,352

LONDON

Authority	Name of Central Medical Adviser	Name of Central Dental Adviser	
Inner London	A. B. Stewart ..	K. C. B. Webster ..	

Authority	Name of Principal School Medical Officer	Name of Principal School Dental Officer	No. of Pupils on Registers January 1968
Inner London Boroughs			
Camden	W. G. Harding ..	G. P. Mailer	22,903
Greenwich.. ..	J. K. Brown	F. Elston	38,928
Hackney	R. G. Davies	S. Gelbier	35,877
Hammersmith	A. D. C. S. Cameron	C. Howard	26,505
Islington	S. King	R. E. Hyman	35,027
Royal Borough of			
Kensington and Chelsea	J. H. Weir	M. C. Downer ..	17,385
Lambeth	A. L. Thrower ..	B. M. Spalding ..	46,290
Lewisham	F. R. Waldron ..	Miss E. Mahler ..	42,389
Southwark	J. E. Epsom	J. J. Cleary	49,123
Tower Hamlets	R. W. Watton ..	D. F. Waller	33,759
Wandsworth	J. T. R. Lewis ..	A. F. Weedon ..	46,500
City of Westminster ..	J. H. Briscoe-Smith ..	R. E. Kean	21,950
City of London	W. G. Swan	L. J. Wallace	264
Outer London Boroughs			
Barking	J. A. Gillett	J. K. Whitelaw ..	27,755
Barnet	D. M. Watkins ..	R. L. James	41,470
Bexley	H. L. Settle	J. H. Forrester ..	32,243
Brent	E. Grundy	A. D. Henderson ..	38,328
Bromley	L. R. Edwards ..	Mrs. C. M. Lindsay ..	43,722
Croydon	S. L. Wright	J. D. Palmer	49,020
Ealing	I. M. Seppelt ..	L. C. Mandeville ..	40,592
Enfield	W. D. Hyde	E. Underhill	37,305
Haringey	J. L. Patton	G. C. H. Kramer ..	34,391
Harrow	W. Cormack	A. G. Brown	27,412
Havering	F. Groarke	E. B. Hodgson ..	42,573
Hillingdon..	O. C. Dobson ..	G. M. Davie	36,192
Hounslow	R. L. Lindon ..	D. H. Norman ..	29,411

Authority	Name of Principal School Medical Officer	Name of Principal School Dental Officer	No. of Pupils on Registers January, 1968
Kingston-upon-Thames ..	J. C. Birchall	D. N. Dodd	18,367
Merton	P. J. Doody	M. T. Gibb	24,555
Newham	F. R. Dennison ..	P. A. Chandler ..	39,243
Redbridge	I. Gordon	E. V. Haigh	31,364
Richmond-upon-Thames	A. M. Nelson ..	G. H. Tucker ..	20,187
Sutton	P. Westcombe ..	Mrs. B. M. Stewart ..	19,978
Waltham Forest	E. W. Wright ..	G. P. L. Taylor ..	30,169

WALES (COUNTIES)

Local Education Authority	Name of Principal School Medical Officer	Name of Principal School Dental Officer	No. of Pupils on Registers January, 1968
Anglesey	G. Crompton.. ..	O. C. Jenkins ..	10,570
Breconshire	D. R. G. Evans ..	J. H. Sutcliffe.. ..	9,230
Caernarvonshire	D. E. Parry-Pritchard	P. J. Frost	18,693
Cardiganshire	I. M. Watkin ..	W. D. P. Evans, J.P.	8,864
Carmarthenshire	D. G. G. Jones ..	W. E. T. Llewelyn ..	26,605
Denbighshire	M. T. I. Jones ..	D. R. Pearse	29,357
Flintshire	G. W. Roberts ..	A. Fielding	28,669
Glamorgan	W. E. Thomas ..	D. R. Edwards ..	131,063
Merioneth	E. Richards	E. C. Jones	6,323
Monmouthshire	A. J. Essex-Cater ..	E. F. J. Sumner ..	61,365
Montgomeryshire ..	E. S. Lovegreen ..	J. A. Reece	7,376
Pembrokeshire	D. J. Davies	D. G. James	18,020
Radnorshire	F. J. H. Crawford ..	P. G. H. Griffith ..	2,953

WALES (COUNTY BOROUGHS)

Local Education Authority	Name of Principal School Medical Officer	Name of Principal School Dental Officer	No. of Pupils on Registers January, 1968
Cardiff	W. P. Phillips.. ..	H. V. Newcombe ..	50,733
Merthyr Tydfil	R. M. Williams ..	F. S. S. Baguley ..	9,890
Newport (Mon.)	W. Burns Clark ..	W. G. Clarkson ..	20,091
Swansea	E. B. Meyrick ..	T. A. Williams ..	28,633

Printed in England for Her Majesty's Stationery Office by McCorquodale & Co. Ltd., London.
H.M. 3513.   Dd. 153496.   K 44.   11/69.   McC. 3309